The
Buddha's
Teachings
As Philosophy

The Buddha's Teachings As Philosophy

Mark Siderits

Hackett Publishing Company, Inc.
Indianapolis/Cambridge

25 24 23 22   1 2 3 4 5 6 7

For further information, please address
   Hackett Publishing Company, Inc.
   P.O. Box 44937
   Indianapolis, Indiana 46244-0937

   www.hackettpublishing.com

Cover design by E. L. Wilson
Interior design by E. L. Wilson
Composition by Aptara, Inc.

Library of Congress Control Number: 2021950343

ISBN-13: 978-1-64792-067-8 (cloth)
ISBN-13: 978-1-64792-066-1 (pbk.)
ISBN-13: 978-1-64792-068-5 (PDF ebook)

The paper used in this publication meets the minimum requirements of
American National Standard for Information Sciences—Permanence of
Paper for Printed Library Materials, ANSI Z39.48–1984.

∞

Contents

About This Book

The Buddha's Teachings As Philosophy was written to fill a particular pedagogical niche: to serve as a text that could be used in undergraduate philosophy or religious studies courses where the instructor wants to broaden the content by including some discussion of the Buddhist philosophical tradition. We certainly hope that it will also be of some interest to readers other than the students in such courses and their instructors. But a few words may be in order at the outset about how it might best be used in the classroom by indicating what it does and does not try to do.

The first point that should be clarified is the scope of the book. The Buddhist philosophical tradition began with the Buddha, developed in South Asia for another one and a half millennia, but also spread to Southeast Asia, Tibet, and East Asia, and continues to develop today. This book treats only the South Asian part of the tradition, and it discusses only the beginnings of the Indian Buddhist tradition—the philosophical elaboration of the Buddha's basic teachings—in any detail. This does provide necessary background for investigating later parts of the Indian tradition, as well as Buddhist thought outside India. But even a whole course could not begin to do justice to the entirety of the Buddhist philosophical tradition. (The much longer *Buddhism As Philosophy*, from which much of the present material is derived, is meant to fill that role for a course wholly devoted to Indian Buddhist philosophy.) A text designed for just one module of a course must keep its focus narrow if it is to achieve the depth necessary for the study of philosophy. But some of the entries in the Further Readings sections at the end of each chapter (especially Chapter 4) are meant to point the interested student in the right direction.

Many of the basic texts of the Buddhist philosophical tradition have now been translated, but even the best translations of the tradition's primary sources can be difficult for the uninitiated to follow. Chapters 2 and 3 use excerpts from some of these sources in order to introduce students to key Buddhist concepts and arguments. Because many students find these texts challenging, the excerpts are followed by fairly extensive elaborations. The pedagogical aim here is, of course, to help students develop the ability to read and understand such texts on their own. Some instructors may wish to go one step further and have students read and try to come to grips with the original sources without reliance on the sorts of elaborations that are presented here. For that reason, the final section of the book, Supplementary Source Readings, contains excerpts from translations of original sources accompanied by no more than the occasional footnote to explain a key technical term. There are readings for each of Chapters 1 through 4, in each case treating a topic that was at least touched on in the relevant chapter. Some instructors may want to use these readings to probe and possibly deepen their students' engagement with the material.

Recent years have seen a substantial increase in scholarship focused on Indian Buddhist philosophy. Not surprisingly, this has meant the emergence of scholarly disagreements concerning the best interpretation of this or that Buddhist philosophical text, theory, or doctrine. There have been disagreements over such matters as whether the Yogācāra school of Mahāyāna Buddhism is a form of idealism (external-world anti-realism), and whether any Buddhist philosophers hold that a contradictory statement can be true. Those disagreements will not be discussed here. The interpretive line followed here is, we think, defensible. But its defense is probably best left to the pages of the relevant scholarly journals. Students might be interested to learn that there are other ways to read parts of the tradition than the ones presented here. We felt, though, that substantive discussion of the interpretive disagreements among scholars might prove distracting at this comparatively early stage in student explorations.

At certain points in the book, there are comparisons of a Buddhist philosophical concept, theory, or argument with something in the Western tradition. Such comparisons are only to be expected in courses that are not devoted exclusively to the Buddhist tradition. But they are sometimes taken amiss by scholars of the Buddhist tradition, who may take them to indicate a Eurocentric bias when it comes to determining what counts as philosophy. Nothing could be further from the truth about their use here. We think it will be evident to anyone who examines the Buddhist corpus that its authors are engaged in philosophical inquiry; special pleading is not necessary. Comparisons of this sort are provided simply because they may be pedagogically useful in one sort of course this book was designed for.

Preparation of *The Buddha's Teachings As Philosophy* would not have been possible without the help and encouragement of Jeff Dean and the publishing team of Hackett Publishing. My thanks go as well to those who had useful suggestions, including Matthew Dasti, Laura Guerrero, Malcolm Keating, Karsten Struhl, Jan Westerhoff, and two anonymous reviewers for Hackett Publishing. Needless to say, any remaining defects are due only to the beginningless ignorance of *this* causal series.

Abbreviations and Translation Sources, Pronunciation

Abbreviations

BCA: *The Bodhicāryāvatāra of Śāntideva with the Commentary Pañjika of Prajñā-karamati*, P. L. Vaidya, ed. (Dharbanga: Mithila Institute, 1960).

M: *Majjhima Nikāya*, V. Trenckner, ed. (London: Pali Text Society, 1948–1960).

MP: *Milindapañho*, R. D. Vadekar, ed. (Bombay: Bombay University Publications, 1972).

S: *Saṃyutta Nikāya*, M. Leon Feer, ed., 5 vols (London: Pali Text Society, 1884–1898).

VM: *Visuddhimagga of Buddhaghosâcariya*, Henry Clarke Warren, ed., rev. by Dharmananda Kosambi (Cambridge, MA: Harvard University Press, 1950).

Pronunciation

1. The macron over a vowel ($\bar{a}$, $\bar{\imath}$, $\bar{u}$) indicates that the value of the vowel is doubled in length. So *a* is pronounced like the "u" in "but," while $\bar{a}$ is pronounced like the "a" in "father" and held longer.

2. An *h* after a consonant indicates aspiration: the consonant sound is followed by a small puff of air. So *th* is not pronounced like the "th" in "the," but rather like the "th" in "warthog."

3. Both *c* and *ch* are pronounced roughly like the "ch" in "cherry," but the *c* is pronounced without aspiration.

4. The three sibilants *s*, *ś*, and *ṣ*: the first is pronounced like the English "s," the second and third roughly like the English "sh."

5. There are no pitch or tonal accents in Sanskrit, but stress accents of three- and four-syllable words work roughly as follows:

If the penultimate syllable has a long vowel, e.g., the *kā* in *Nikāya*, stress falls on the penultimate syllable: ni-KĀ-ya.

If the penultimate syllable has a short vowel, e.g., the *ju* in Nāgārjuna or the *la* in Himālaya, the stress falls on the preceding syllable: nā-GĀR-ju-na, hi-MĀ-la-ya.

For more details on Sanskrit pronunciation see the "Pronunciation of Sanskrit words" page on the Rigpa Shedra Wiki website at https://www.rigpawiki.org/index.php?title=Pronunciation_of_ Sanskrit_words.

Introduction

Buddhism As Philosophy?

The purpose of this book is, as the title suggests, to examine the Buddha's teachings—the core of Buddhism—as philosophy. Before we actually start doing that, though, it might be good to first get a bit clearer about what each of these two things—Buddhism and philosophy—is. That will help us see what might be distinctive about studying Buddhism as a form of philosophy. And it is important to be clear about this since there are some preconceptions about these matters that might get in the way of fully grasping how the philosophical study of Buddhism works.

I.1 What Is Philosophy?

When people first encounter philosophy, they want to know what it is about. Other disciplines have their own subject matter: biology is the study of life processes, sociology is the study of human societies, astronomy looks at planets and stars, and so on. So what is philosophy about? If you are not new to the study of philosophy, you know that what makes philosophy a separate discipline is not necessarily its special subject matter. True, there are questions that we naturally think of as "philosophical" in some sense. Questions such as, "How should I live my life?" and "How do we know anything?" and "How did all this come to be?" But the first question is also addressed by literature, the second by cognitive science, and the third by astrophysics. What distinguishes philosophy from other disciplines?

Someone who has already studied philosophy will also know that the answer has more to do with method than with content. What sets philosophy apart as a discipline is more its concern with how to answer questions than with the answers themselves. To study philosophy is to learn to think carefully and critically about complex issues. It is not necessarily to learn "the answers" that the discipline has arrived at. This can make the study of philosophy frustrating for some. When we first study a subject, we expect to learn the body of knowledge that has been developed by that discipline. When we study chemistry, we learn the atomic weights of the elements, when we study history, we learn the causes of the First World War, and so on. Only later, if at all, does one start looking into the methods the discipline uses within its field of knowledge. The study of philosophy is not like that. True, one might find out in an introductory philosophy course that Plato thought the soul must be immortal or that Descartes held the one thing that can't be doubted is that the "I" exists. But one also learns that not all philosophers agree with Plato or Descartes on these claims. Some students find this immensely frustrating. Where, they want to know, are the facts that philosophy has established? In all the centuries that philosophy has existed, has it made any progress, come up with any answers?

One response to this question is that indeed philosophy has established something quite significant—that the truth turns out to be very complicated. None of the simple answers to the questions that philosophy looks at is correct. This is an important (and unsettling) result. The questions that philosophers ask often seem like they should have simple and straightforward answers. Take, for instance, the question of how the mind and the body interact. The state of my stomach causes me to think about what there is to eat, and then the resulting state of my mind brings about bodily motion in the direction of the refrigerator. How do these things happen? One thing that philosophical investigation of this question has shown is that we still don't know the answer. Even more detailed scientific study of the brain won't succeed (at least by itself) in explaining how this works. Yet, we rely on the mind and the body working together in everything we do. So perhaps philosophy has established something after all—that under the surface of seemingly mundane matters lurks surprising complexity. Getting to the bottom of things turns out to be really hard work.

But there is another way to answer the complaint that philosophy hasn't established any facts. Someone who says this might be wondering what the point of studying philosophy is. And the way the challenge is posed suggests that they think the point of studying some subject is to acquire a body of knowledge—to add new facts to the facts they already know. So one response to the challenge might be to question this assumption. Perhaps the point (or at least a point) of studying philosophy is to acquire a set of skills. Specifically, the study of philosophy might turn out to be one of the best ways to learn some critical argumentation skills: defining one's terms carefully, constructing good arguments in support of one's views, critically evaluating arguments (one's own and others'), responding to objections, and the like.[1] And these skills turn out to play a crucial role in many different areas of life. They are, for instance, extremely important to the practice of law. This would explain why the study of philosophy is recognized as one of the best ways to prepare for legal practice (something that was known in ancient Greece and in medieval India). Of course, the issues that philosophers grapple with can be intrinsically interesting to anyone who is at all thoughtful and reflective. But on this way of thinking about philosophy, the benefit of grappling with them is not so

---

1. A note about the word "argument." As philosophers use this term, an argument is just a presentation of evidence that is meant to support some conclusion. An argument always consists of two or more statements: a conclusion and one or more premises. The conclusion is the statement that the author of the argument is trying to get the audience to accept. The premises are statements that the author thinks the audience is likely to already accept, and that the author thinks will show that the conclusion is more likely to be true. Giving an argument is one way of trying to persuade others of something. It differs from other forms of persuasion in that when it is properly done it engages the rationality of the audience—it leaves it up to them to determine whether or not they've been given good reasons to accept the conclusion.

much that one gets the "right" answer, as that one learns to think more carefully and critically about complex matters in general.

To say this is not to say that the questions that philosophers ask are unimportant. Because people find these to be pressing questions, they pursue the difficult task of trying to answer them, thereby developing their logical and analytical skills. So something more should be said at this point about what sorts of questions these are. Philosophical inquiry can be sorted into several broad areas. One such domain is ethics. This has to do with the general question of how we should live our lives. So it includes not just questions about the nature of morality (which is concerned with what constitutes right and wrong in the treatment of others). It also deals with questions about what sort of life might be the best life for persons. Now it is sometimes thought that questions of ethics and morality are questions for religion. And it is true that most religions have a great deal to say on these matters. But when people think of questions of right and wrong, good and bad, as matters for religion, they often have in mind the idea that a religion simply tells us how we ought to behave. So they are thinking of ethics and morality as a set of rules or commandments. This is not what philosophers mean by ethics, though. As they use the term, ethics involves critical examination of competing views about how we ought to conduct ourselves. And this is something that one can do regardless of what (if any) religious beliefs someone has. The medieval Christian thinker Thomas Aquinas was doing ethics in this sense when he tried to determine what conclusions we can draw about being virtuous from a certain view of human nature. But so was the nineteenth century German atheist Friedrich Nietzsche when he asked how we should live our lives given that God is dead. What makes both their discussions of ethical matters philosophical is that both involve the critical examination of arguments.

Metaphysics is another major area of philosophy. The word "metaphysics" gets used in several different ways. For instance, in bookstores, the "metaphysics" section often has books on astrology and the occult.

But as it is used in philosophy, it simply refers to the disciplined investigation of the most basic features of reality. Where ethics concerns the
question of how things ought to be, metaphysics concerns the question
of how things fundamentally are, or what reality is basically like. Now
we might think that questions about how things are, or what reality is
like, should be left to the sciences. And it is true that if, for instance, we
wanted to know what a certain chemical compound is like, we should
turn to chemistry. But metaphysical questions are much more basic or
fundamental than those that science can answer. Chemistry can tell
us what effects might be caused by mixing two chemicals. But it is a
metaphysical question what the general nature of the relation between
cause and effect is. Likewise the sciences tell us a great deal about the
nature of the physical world. But it is a metaphysical question whether
everything that exists is physical; this is not a question that scientists
can or should try to answer using the methods of science. Some other
examples of metaphysical questions include: What is the nature of
time? Are there, in addition to particulars such as individual cows,
universals such as a single cowness that exists in all of them simultaneously? Does there exist an all-perfect, eternal creator of the universe?
Is there a self, and if so, what might it be like? The pursuit of metaphysical questions like these has often led philosophers to related but
separate questions in the philosophy of language, such as how it is that
words and sentences have meaning, and what it means for a statement
to be true.

   Another important area of philosophy is epistemology or the theory of knowledge. Here the basic question is how we can come to know
what things are like and what should be done. Inquiry in epistemology
has often taken the form of asking just what it means to say that someone knows something or other. For instance, can someone be said to
know something if they haven't ruled out all the ways in which they
could be mistaken (even when they're not mistaken)? But epistemological inquiry may also take the form of asking what are the means or
methods of knowledge. Sense-perception and inference (or reasoning)

are popular candidates for reliable ways to acquire knowledge, but what about authority (taking the word of some trustworthy person) or reasoning by analogy? And if there are different means of knowledge, how are they related to one another? Does each have its own distinctive sphere, or do they all serve equally well to give us knowledge about the same objects? Does any one means of knowledge have precedence over others?

As you might have guessed given what was said earlier about the nature of philosophy, philosophers have developed a number of different theories in each of its different branches. And there is no general consensus as to which theories in metaphysics, epistemology, and ethics are correct. There is general agreement that the simplest answers are wrong. Take, for instance, the ethical theory of subject-based ethical relativism. This is the view that whether an action is morally wrong for someone to do depends on whether or not they sincerely believe that doing it is wrong. All philosophers today would agree that this theory is false. But when it comes to more sophisticated theories in these areas, agreement breaks down. For every theory that has been proposed in metaphysics, epistemology, and ethics, there are serious criticisms that have been developed by philosophers. Much of the practice of philosophy involves looking at these objections to a given view and seeing if it's possible to answer them. (It is through this process that philosophical theories have grown so sophisticated.) But in doing so, one frequently discovers that there are important connections between the view one holds in one area of philosophy and the positions one takes in other areas. A particular theory in ethics might, for instance, turn out to be unworkable unless one holds a certain position on some metaphysical issue. Learning to see these sorts of connections is another important benefit of studying philosophy.

Not every culture developed its own philosophical tradition. But ancient Greece did—this is where modern Western philosophy began. And so did classical India. In each case, the original impetus seems to have come from a concern to answer ethical questions. Out of dissatisfaction with the received view of how people should live their lives, there arose efforts at thinking systematically about these matters. But in both cases, these inquiries soon led to major developments in metaphysics and epistemology. For philosophers became aware that if we are to make progress toward determining how we ought to live, we need to be clearer about the nature of the world and our place in it. And this, in turn, requires greater clarity about what constitutes knowledge and what processes lead to it. People sometimes wonder if it could be just a coincidence that philosophy arose in two such different cultures at roughly the same time. Now we know that there were trade contacts between classical India and the Hellenic world. So it is at least conceivable that some ancient Greek philosophers and some classical Indian philosophers knew something of one another's work. But the two philosophical traditions appear to be genuinely distinct. They tackle the same basic questions in ethics, metaphysics, and epistemology. And they employ the same basic techniques of analysis and argumentation. Sometimes individual philosophers in the two traditions even reach strikingly similar conclusions. But this should not lead us to suppose that there was significant borrowing between one tradition and the other. We know, after all, that the same invention can occur independently in two distinct cultures. In mathematics, for instance, the zero was invented separately, in ancient India and also by the Mayans of precontact Mesoamerica.

I.2 What Is Buddhism?

Philosophy, then, is the systematic investigation of questions in ethics, metaphysics, and epistemology (as well as several related fields). It involves using analysis and argumentation in systematic and reflective ways. This will do, at least for now, as an account of what we will mean by philosophy. What about the other term in our title, the Buddha's thought? We might seem to be on safer ground here. While many people might lack detailed knowledge about what it is that Buddhists believe and what Buddhist practice involves, surely everyone knows that Buddhism is the religion that was founded in ancient India by the Buddha, subsequently spread throughout Asia, and is now attracting adherents in the West? Well, yes, but there's a load of mischief lurking in that word "religion." There is one sense in which Buddhism can accurately be called a religion, but there is another sense in which it would be a mistake. And clarity about this matter will prove just as crucial to our undertaking as will being clear about what philosophy is.

We often base our understanding of a word on familiar examples. In the case of "religion," the familiar examples for most people in the West are Christianity, Judaism, and Islam. These are all monotheistic religions: they each involve belief in a single personal being who is eternal, is creator of the universe, and has all perfections. Not all religions share this sort of belief: Hinduism and Shinto are both forms of polytheism. It doesn't seem to be stretching things too much to group all the theisms under one label, though. But particularly if the religion one is most familiar with is Christianity, one might also think of a religion as a "faith." To think of religion this way is to see it as a set of beliefs that one accepts out of a conviction that is not based on rational argument. Religion is then seen as falling on the "heart" side of the head/heart, or reason/faith, divide.

In modern Western culture, there is a tendency to suppose that certain questions are to be settled through the use of reason, while others can only be addressed through faith and feeling. This is the dichotomy between reason and faith, with reason seen as a matter of the head and faith a matter of the heart. Along with this dichotomy, there is a related one between facts, seen as the sort of thing that the sciences discover, and values, seen as private, subjective commitments that are not open to rational investigation and scrutiny. Suppose we agree that using our reason involves thinking about things in a cool, careful, detached, and deliberate way. Now it is probably true that some matters should not be decided entirely on the basis of calm, cool consideration of reasons. One's choice of life partner, for instance, should probably involve considerable input from the "heart" side. But it is not at all clear that "head" and "heart" constitute a strict dichotomy. And in any event, it is not obvious that the matters we consider religious (or "spiritual") necessarily belong on the "faith" side of any such divide.

One thing that all the theisms (monotheisms and polytheisms) have in common is that they each try to articulate some vision of the ideal state for humans. This ideal state is usually depicted as being quite different from the way that people would live their lives if left to their own devices. The latter "mundane" (or "worldly") state is depicted as inherently unsatisfactory, as fallen away from how we ought to be. And the ideal state is represented as a sort of salvation from this fallen state. When we think of a religion as dealing with "spiritual" matters, it is this concern with attaining salvation, of escaping from an unsatisfactory way of being, that we have in mind. The concerns of religion are, in a word, soteriological. (A soteriology is a doctrine of salvation.) Now to think of religion as a faith is to suppose that soteriological concerns can only be addressed through a form of emotional commitment. It is to hold that the use of reason or logical investigation is of little or no use in seeking salvation. Many people in our culture believe this. But this was not the view of classical Indian culture. (Nor does it seem to have been held by the ancient Greeks or by the philosophers of medieval Islam.) To many people in ancient India, including the Buddha, it made perfectly good sense to use our rational faculties in the pursuit of salvation. Of course, this was not the only path that Indians recognized. According to the Bhagavad Gītā (a Hindu text), there are four such paths, and which path one should follow depends on one's talents and predilections.[2] But all four paths are said to bring about salvation by instilling knowledge of our true identity. The Buddha taught that

---

2. The four are the path of detached duty, the path of meditation, the path of knowledge, and the path of devotion.

there is just one path to liberation, not four. But that path consists in the combined practice of philosophical reasoning and meditation. Indian Buddhists, like others in ancient India, thought that salvation from our unsatisfactory state was to be had through coming to know the truth about who we are and where we fit in the universe. And they thought that attaining such insights requires the use of philosophical rationality.[3]

Buddhism is, then, a religion, if by this we mean a set of teachings that address soteriological concerns. But if we think of religion as a kind of faith, a commitment for which no reasons can be given, then Buddhism would not count. To become a Buddhist is not to accept a bundle of doctrines solely on the basis of faith. And salvation is not to be had just by devout belief in the Buddha's teachings. (Indeed, the Buddhists we will study would be likely to see belief of this sort as an obstacle to final liberation.) Rather, liberation, or nirvāna (to use the Buddhist term), is to be attained through rational investigation of the nature of the world. As we would expect with any religion, Buddhist teachings include some claims that run deeply counter to common sense. But Buddhists are not expected to accept these claims just because the Buddha taught them. Instead, they are expected to examine the arguments that are given in support of these claims, and determine for themselves if the arguments really make it likely that these claims are true. Buddhists revere the Buddha as the founder of their tradition. But that attitude is meant to be the same as what is accorded a teacher who has discovered important truths through their

---

3. This is not to say that Buddhism is a philosophy and not a religion. To say that would be to assume that it must be one or the other, that there is a strict dichotomy between reason and faith. Many Buddhists would reject that assumption. Their attitude toward soteriological matters might be usefully compared to one we often take today toward scientific matters. Most of us who are not scientists tend to take the more advanced theories of a science like physics on trust. But we know that if we were to receive proper training, we would be able to assess for ourselves the evidence in support of those theories.

own intellectual power. Indeed the person whom we call the Buddha, Gautama,[4] is said to have been just the latest in a long series of buddhas, each of whom independently discovered the same basic truths that show the way to nirvāna.[5] This may or may not reflect historical fact. But the spirit behind this claim is worth remarking on. It seems to suggest that the teachings of Buddhism are based on objective facts about the nature of reality and our place in it. And these facts are apparently thought of as things that human reason can apprehend without reliance on superhuman revelation.

If we expect all religions to be theistic, then Buddhism might once again not qualify as a religion. The Buddha is not the equivalent of the God of Western monotheism. Nor is the Buddha considered a prophet, someone whose authority on spiritual matters derives from privileged access to God. Gautama is seen as just an extremely intelligent and altruistic human being. Indeed Buddhism explicitly denies that there is such a thing as the God recognized by Western monotheism—an eternal, all-powerful, and all-perfect creator. To most people, this denial is tantamount to atheism. So if we are to count Buddhism as a religion, it will have to make sense to say there can be atheistic religions.

---

4. "Gautama" is the Sanskrit version of his name, "Gotama" the Pāli version. In addition, there are a number of epithets that are used to refer to him: "Śākyamuni" ("sage of the Śākya clan"), "Siddhārtha" ("one whose aim is accomplished"), and "Tathāgata" ("one who has thus gone") are among the more common. "Buddha" is not a name or epithet but a title: a buddha is someone who has independently discovered the facts about suffering, its causes and its cure, and taught these to the world. Becoming a buddha supposedly involves a long and arduous process of preparation. Someone who has chosen to enter into that process but has not yet arrived at the destination of buddhahood is referred to as a bodhisattva (a "being [destined for] enlightenment").
5. Buddhists believe that everything that arises through causal conditions is impermanent. This would include the teachings developed by Gautama and transmitted through the Buddhist tradition. So eventually, these teachings will disappear. Facts like those that Gautama recognized will continue to obtain, however. Thus in time, another buddha may come along and recognize the significance of such facts for human salvation. This has supposedly happened many times in the past.

Of course, the Buddha acknowledged the existence of a multiplicity of gods. Should we then think of Buddhism as polytheistic, in the same sense in which some forms of Hinduism are polytheistic?[6] Perhaps we might if we wanted Buddhism to fit under a nice tidy definition of "religion" that required some form of theism. But this would be somewhat beside the point as far as Buddhism is concerned. The gods that ancient Indian Buddhists believed in were (like the gods of ancient Greece and all the rest of pre-Christian Europe) finite beings, rather like human beings, only longer-lived and more powerful. More importantly, they play no role whatsoever in the quest for nirvāna. Perhaps worship and sacrifice to the right gods might win one various mundane benefits, such as timely rainfall to make the crops grow or the health of one's loved ones. But the gods cannot bestow nirvāna on us. Indeed the fact that they are also mortal (they may live for unimaginably long periods, but they are still impermanent like everything else) is taken to show that they are no more enlightened than we humans are. For that matter, even an enlightened human being like a buddha or an *arhat* (someone who has attained nirvāna by following the teachings of the Buddha) cannot bestow nirvāna on others. That is something that one can only attain for oneself; enlightened beings can only help others by giving them pointers along the way. And the point, for Buddhism, is to attain nirvāna, to bring suffering to an end. So for this spiritual tradition, the question of whether there are any gods turns out to be largely irrelevant.

The doctrine of karma and rebirth is another matter. As you may well already know, classical Indian Buddhism accepted this doctrine. These Buddhists believed that death is ordinarily not the end of our existence, that after we die, we are reborn, either as humans or as some other form of sentient being (including non-human animals, gods, and

---

6. Indeed, many of the same gods that we find in classical Hindu texts show up in the Indian Buddhist tradition as well. See A. K. Warder, *Indian Buddhism* (Delhi: Motilal Banarsidass), 1970, pp. 152–56.

the inhabitants of various hells). Which sort of rebirth one attains depends on your karma, which has to do with the moral quality of the actions you engaged in. If one's acts were primarily morally good, one might be reborn as a human in fortunate life circumstances or even as a god. If one's life was full of acts done out of evil intentions, however, one might end up as a *preta* or so-called hungry ghost (so called because everything they can eat tastes like feces). Now to many ears, this will sound like just the sort of thing that other more familiar religions offer: a promise of life after death and a doctrine of retribution for one's sins. So is Buddhism really all that different from those other spiritual traditions? Is it really the case that it only expects us to believe those things for which there is objective evidence?

This is a good question. It may turn out that not everything Buddhists have traditionally believed can be rationally supported. This outcome is one of the possibilities that open up when we examine Buddhism as philosophy. But before saying any more about that, we should clear up some possible confusions about the doctrine of karma and rebirth. The first point to make is that as Buddhists understand it, karma is not divine retribution for one's sins. You may have noticed that the laws of karma basically have to do with receiving pleasant results for acting out of morally good motives and receiving painful results for acting with evil intentions. This prompts some to ask who determines what is good and what is evil. For Buddhists, the answer is that no one does. Karma is not a set of rules that are decreed by a cosmic ruler and enforced by the cosmic moral police. Karma is understood instead as a set of impersonal causal laws that simply describe how the world happens to work. In this respect, the karmic laws are just like the so-called natural laws that science investigates. It is a causal law that when I let go of a rock while standing on a bridge, it will fall toward the water below with a certain acceleration. No one passed this law, and no one enforces it. The laws of physics are not like the laws passed by legislative bodies. There are no gravity cops. And if something were to behave contrary to what we take to be the law of gravity, that would be evidence that we were wrong to think it was a law. A true causal law has no exceptions. Likewise, the laws of karma are understood not as rules that can be either obeyed or broken, but as exceptionless generalizations about what always follows what. If we could keep track of enough persons over enough successive lives, we could find out what the laws of karma are in the same way that science discovers what the laws of nature are: our observations would disclose the patterns of regular succession that show causation at work.[7]

A second point to make about the Buddhist attitude toward karma and rebirth is that belief in rebirth does not serve the same function that belief in an afterlife serves in many other religious traditions. The fact that after I die I will be reborn is not taken to be a source of relief or consolation. And the point of Buddhist practice is not to do those things that will help ensure a pleasant next life and prevent a painful one. The truth is just the opposite. As we will see in more detail in Chapter 1, the Buddha claims that continued rebirth is just what we need liberation from. (The reason, briefly, is that rebirth entails redeath.[8]) One could set about trying to use knowledge of

---

7. It is widely held not just by Buddhists but by other classical Indian schools as well that the practice of meditation or *yoga* leads to the development of a number of extraordinary powers. One that is frequently mentioned is the ability to recall past lives, first of oneself and then of others. Someone who had such powers could tell us what the karmic causal laws actually are, for they would be able to observe which deeds in one life were regularly followed by pleasant rebirths, which by painful rebirths. Since every intentional act has some karmic effect, the patterns would be quite complex and difficult to discern. But it could at least in principle be done.

8. Buddhism shares with other Indian schools the view that continued rebirth is unsatisfactory and something from which we should seek liberation. The idea that rebirth is unsatisfactory because it means repeated death is expressed in several passages in two of the earlier Upaniṣads. (See Robert E. Hume, trans., *The Thirteen Principal Upanishads* [Oxford: Oxford University Press, 1931], pp. 143, 355.) While some of the Upaniṣads were composed after the time of the Buddha, most scholars consider these particular passages to predate the Buddha.

karmic causal laws to try to guarantee that one continues to exist in relatively comfortable circumstances. But on the Buddhist analysis, that would just reveal one's ignorance about how things really are. And because such behavior was based on ignorance, it would inevitably lead to more of the suffering that Buddhism is meant to cure. The doctrine of karma and rebirth is not meant to make us feel better about the fact that we will die. For those Buddhists who accept it, it is part of the problem, not part of the solution.

A third point about the doctrine of karma and rebirth is that this was not a view that was peculiar to Buddhism. Instead, it seems to have been commonly accepted by spiritual teachers from before the time of the Buddha, and to have been part of the commonsense conception of the world for most Indians for most of the time that Buddhism existed in India. So when Indian Buddhists claimed that we undergo rebirth in accordance with karma, they were not making claims that would have struck their audience as novel or strange. Now when we think of a religion as something that makes claims that must be taken on faith, we have in mind claims that are not already part of common sense. So the fact that Buddhists accepted the doctrine of karma and rebirth does not show that Buddhism is a religion in the sense of a creed, a set of doctrines for which there is no evidence and that are to be accepted on faith. Perhaps Indians accepted this doctrine without good evidence. But if so, it was not because they were required to as practicing Buddhists.

The doctrine of karma and rebirth is not a part of our commonsense worldview. So it would be reasonable for us to ask what evidence there is that this doctrine is true. It would be reasonable, that is, if we are investigating Buddhism as philosophy. For in studying philosophy, we are interested in finding out what the truth is. (We may not always find it, but that's what we aim for.) Things might be different if we were studying Buddhism as a historical artifact, as part of the study of the history of religions. Perhaps then we would simply note that Indian Buddhists believed in karma and rebirth, and set aside the question whether they were justified in their belief. Instead, we might simply explore how this belief affected other aspects of Buddhism: their ethical teachings, for instance, or the content of their artistic representations. There is a great deal we can learn by studying Buddhism and other religions in this way. By simply setting aside the question whether the teachings are true or false, and focusing on how different elements of the tradition might be related to one another, we can learn to see Buddhism's inner logic, how it hangs together as a system. This can help us see things we might otherwise miss. But it cannot tell us whether its teachings are reasonable. And this is something we might want to know when we study a religion like Buddhism. Buddhists claim that those of their teachings that run counter to common sense can be supported by rational arguments. Are they right about this? And if it turns out that some claim of theirs that strikes us as strange cannot be given rational support, how much damage does that do to the overall system? These are the sorts of questions that philosophical examination involves.

And this is how we will proceed with the doctrine of karma and rebirth (and with some other equally controversial views). We will ask (among other things) if there are good reasons to believe it. If there are not, we will go on to see whether other important teachings of Buddhism would also have to go if this doctrine were thrown overboard. This might come as a shock, particularly if you think of a person's religion as something sacrosanct that others shouldn't question. How can we criticize beliefs that might turn out to be central to another person's whole way of life? But someone who asks this is forgetting something: Buddhist philosophers thought that their most important claims should be subjected to rational investigation. This is what made them philosophers. They certainly criticized the views of other Buddhist philosophers. And there was a great deal of rational criticism exchanged between the Buddhists and other Indian philosophers. So perhaps it would actually be dishonoring Buddhism not to subject its doctrines to rational scrutiny. To study it as no more than an item of historical interest, and not ask how much truth there is in its core teachings, might mean failing to take it seriously as an important human creation.

I.3 Examining Buddhism As Philosophy

We have said enough for now about what philosophy is and what Buddhism is. And we have already begun to discuss what it might mean to study Buddhism as philosophy. There are a number of other things that need to be said on that score. One is that this study will be selective. Like any other religious tradition, Buddhism is an immensely complicated phenomenon. To study Buddhism as philosophy means primarily studying texts. Specifically, it means studying those Buddhist texts that present philosophical theories and arguments. But this means leaving out of consideration many other sorts of Buddhist writings, such as those that specify the rules that monks and nuns must follow when they enter the Buddhist monastic order (the *saṃgha*), and those more popular writings designed to present simple moral teachings to an audience of lay followers. Moreover, there is much more to Buddhism than its literature (huge though that literature is). And our focus on texts means these other areas will go largely untouched. We will not be examining the many different kinds of Buddhist artistic expression to be found in such fields as sculpture, architecture, painting, devotional poetry, and drama. We will have very little to say about Buddhist institutions, and their organization and history. We will say very little about the Buddhist practice of meditation and nothing at all about such lay Buddhist devotional practices as stūpa worship. All of these aspects of Buddhism have been dealt with elsewhere, and there is no need to duplicate that scholarship here.[9]

---

9. An excellent resource that discusses many of these topics with respect to Indian Buddhism from its origins to its destruction in the late twelfth century CE is A. K. Warder's *Indian Buddhism*.

There are, though, other studies of Buddhism that focus on many of the same topics that we will be examining. These are works that try to introduce Buddhism through a survey of its chief schools and their principal doctrines. Since such studies are usually organized historically, they might be called doctrinal histories of Buddhism. Now this work will try to trace a historical progression as well. But there will be less concern here than in the typical doctrinal history to say who influenced whom, what influenced what, in the development of key Buddhist teachings. Indeed at times, we will take things out of their historical order. This will happen where understanding conceptual connections takes precedence over working out the historical order in which ideas developed. But the most important difference between this work and doctrinal histories of Buddhism is that the latter are more likely to present just the conclusions of the Buddhist philosophers. Our job will be to look not only at their conclusions, but also at the arguments they gave in support of their conclusions. We will look at the objections that other Indian philosophers raised against the Buddhist views we examine, and we will consider the responses that Buddhists gave. We will try to come up with our own objections and then try to figure out what (if anything) we think Buddhist philosophers could say to answer them. We will try, in short, to see how well Buddhist doctrines stand up to the test of rational scrutiny. Because we are examining Buddhism philosophically, we want to know what (if anything) in Buddhist teachings is true.

Now some of those teachings we can quite easily say are false. This is because some of the claims of Buddhist philosophers are based on views of the natural world very different from what our own sciences tell us about nature. For instance, some Buddhist philosophers hold that ordinary physical objects such as rocks and tables are made up of very large numbers of atoms of four different types: earth, air, water, and fire. (Similar views are found in ancient Greek philosophy.[10]) Now, this idea that material things are made up of four different elements or kinds of stuff is one we know today is false. When ancient philosophers called water an element, they had in mind that there was just one fundamental kind of stuff present in every liquid. So the difference between H_2O and ethyl alcohol might just be a matter of how much fire element was present in addition to the water element. We now know that there are far more than four naturally occurring elements, and two liquids might be made up of completely different elements. Moreover, we know that each of these elements is in turn made up of more fundamental particles, until we reach what may be the most basic of these, the six kinds of quarks. So when Buddhist philosophers argue about a question like whether color is present in each of the four elements, we can say that the very question is misguided—no answer is likely to be true.

Does this mean that Buddhist philosophy can be dismissed as an outdated, prescientific view of the world? No. The situation here is like what we find when we study ancient Greek philosophy. The Greek philosopher Aristotle believed that the earth is the center of the universe. We know that this is false, and yet Aristotle is still considered an important philosopher. What we have learned to do in studying ancient philosophy is simply set aside those parts that conflict with our modern scientific knowledge and focus on what remains. This is a legitimate approach. When philosophy began, both in ancient Greece and in ancient India, it was felt that philosophers ought to develop a truly comprehensive worldview. For the same methods of rational analysis and argumentation that philosophers were developing in order to answer questions in metaphysics, epistemology, and ethics,

---

10. Classical Chinese philosophy has a cosmological theory that uses the five terms "wood," "fire," "earth," "metal," and "water." Modern scholars have often interpreted this as a theory of elements like those of classical Greek and Indian philosophy, but some scholars question this interpretation. For discussion, see: A. C. Graham, *Disputers of the Tao* (La Salle, IL: Open Court, 1989), pp. 340–70.

seemed to likewise be suitable for studying the natural world. So for instance, Aristotle wrote treatises on biology and meteorology, and the Sāṃkhya school of Indian philosophy developed a theory of chemistry. Indeed most of our present natural sciences have their origins in philosophy. But they have since developed their own distinctive methods and have become independent disciplines. Philosophy now focuses principally on issues in metaphysics, epistemology, and ethics. (This can lead to philosophical investigation of the natural sciences themselves; but studying the sciences philosophically is different from doing science.) This is why, when we today look at ancient philosophers, we tend to set to one side the details of their views about how the natural world works. For it usually turns out that even when these details are simply wrong, this has little or no effect on their views in the core philosophical areas of metaphysics, epistemology, and ethics. This is how we will treat the Buddhist philosophers as well.

There is another element in the texts we will study that we shall also want to set to one side. What we will be examining are texts in which Buddhists give arguments for, and consider objections to, their key claims in metaphysics, epistemology, and ethics. But in some cases, the reason given to support a claim involves an appeal to the authority of the Buddha. This sort of thing happens when there is a dispute between two different schools of Buddhist philosophy over some doctrine. One school may then point to some passage in the sūtras (the discourses of Gautama and his chief disciples) as grounds for accepting their position. Now, this might count as a good reason to accept the view in question if you already thought that the Buddha's teachings were authoritative. But for those of us who do not, a dispute that is conducted in this way can only concern how to interpret the discourses of the Buddha. The question for us is not whether a certain doctrine is consistent with what the Buddha himself said. The question we want to answer is whether there's reason to think the doctrine is true. Sometimes the texts we will be looking at try to answer both questions. When this happens, we will focus on just their attempts to answer the second.

Most chapters in this book contain extracts from primary sources in Buddhist philosophy, as well as extensive discussion. This means we will be reading passages from a variety of Buddhist philosophical texts, beginning with the sūtras and ending with texts written centuries later. Reading and understanding these texts will pose some real challenges. Because these were mostly written for other classical Indian philosophers, it is not always easy to see what the argument is, and how the author responds to objections. But we will start slowly, and you will have plenty of help on this. The point here is for you to learn to read and understand these texts on your own. That way, if you want to look more deeply into some topic in Buddhist philosophy, you will be able to do so without having to rely on anyone else's interpretation. Then you'll be better equipped to try to find out what the truth is for yourself.

One final point before we begin our study of the Buddha's teachings as philosophy. Some people might take the title of this book to mean that it will tell them what the Buddhist philosophy is. But as you may have guessed by now, there is no such thing as the Buddhist philosophy—at least not in the sense in which we are using "philosophy" here. Given what the discipline of philosophy is, it should not be surprising that Buddhist philosophers disagree among themselves. By the same token, there is no such thing as the Christian philosophy or the Jewish philosophy. There are philosophers who use the tools of philosophy to try to articulate what they take to be the basic truths of Christianity and of Judaism. But Aquinas and Kierkegaard disagree profoundly in their understandings of Christian teachings, and Maimonides and Spinoza likewise differ in how they approach the philosophical expression of Judaism. Things are no different when we come to Buddhism. While there are certain fundamentals on which all Buddhist philosophers agree, there are important issues over which they disagree. Sometimes these differences can make things quite complicated. So to help us keep track of things, it would be useful to have a taxonomy or classification of Buddhist philosophical systems. We can start with this basic division into three distinct phases in the development of Buddhist philosophy:

1. Early Buddhism: the teachings of the Buddha and his immediate disciples;

2. Abhidharma: the development of rigorous metaphysical and epistemological theories growing out of the attempt to give consistent, systematic interpretations of the teachings of Early Buddhism;

3. Mahāyāna: philosophical criticism of aspects of Abhidharma doctrines, together with an alternative account of what Buddhist metaphysics and epistemology should look like.

Both the second and the third phase saw the development of a number of different schools, reflecting different approaches to the challenges being confronted.

We will be looking (in Chapter 4) at just three of these schools, Vaibhāṣika (an Abhidharma school), and Yogācāra and Madhyamaka (two Mahāyāna schools). We will try to see how their views developed out of the Buddha's teachings and get a sense of how their arguments work. But we will begin, in the next three chapters, with the fundamentals that all Buddhist philosophical schools agree on, the basic teachings of Early Buddhism.

Some Key Points of This Chapter

- Philosophy is the investigation of questions in ethics, metaphysics, and epistemology. It involves using reasoned analysis and argumentation in systematic and reflective ways.

- Buddhism may be considered a religion in the sense of being a soteriology, a set of teachings and practices intended to help people overcome the suffering that results from living in accordance with ordinary conceptions of how our lives should go.

- Buddhism is not a religion in the sense of a "faith," a set of beliefs that one must accept solely on the basis of authority.

For Further Reading

As was mentioned in note 9, A. K. Warder's *Indian Buddhism* (Delhi: Motilal Banarsidass, 1970) is an excellent resource for the history of Buddhism in India, particularly the period from its founding through the fifth century CE.

For a discussion of the historical relations between ancient Greek philosophy and classical Indian philosophy see Thomas McEvilley, *The Shape of Ancient Thought* (New York: Allworth Press, 2002).

For discussion of the question of whether the Buddha himself can be considered a philosopher, see Douglass Smith and Justin Whitaker, "Reading the Buddha as a Philosopher," *Philosophy East and West* 66, no. 2 (April 2016): 515–38.

For a brief beginner's introduction to the methods of philosophy (though written from a Western perspective) see Peter S. Fosl and Julian Baggini, *The Philosopher's Toolkit: A Compendium of Philosophical Concepts and Methods*, 3rd ed. (Chichester, UK: Wiley-Blackwell, 2020).

Chapter One
Early Buddhism: Basic Teachings

In this chapter, we will explore the basic teachings of Early Buddhism, the teachings of the Buddha and his immediate disciples. This will serve to introduce a set of core principles that all Buddhist philosophers accept. In a later chapter we will examine how various Buddhist philosophers developed these core teachings in different ways. But before we get to those basic ideas that are common to all schools of Buddhism, it might be useful to say a few words about the life of the Buddha.

1.1 Who Was the Buddha?

Apart from his career as a teacher, there is little that is known with much confidence about the details of Gautama's life. Until recently, scholars were fairly certain that he lived from 566 to 486 BCE. But recent research suggests that his death may have been as late as 404 BCE. So if we accept the traditional claim that he lived for eighty years, then perhaps his life was lived wholly within the fifth century BCE. He was born in the city-state of Kapilavastu, the home of the Śākyas,[1] in what is now the western part of Nepal near the Indian border. He grew up in relatively comfortable circumstances. But in early adulthood, he chose to abandon the settled life of a householder and became a wandering renunciant or *śramaṇa*, someone whose life is dedicated to finding answers to certain spiritual questions.

---

1. Hence the epithet he later acquired, "Śākyamuni," or "sage of the Śākyas."

The *śramaṇa*s of sixth to fifth century India represented a new phenomenon in Indian religious life. They rejected key elements of the prevailing Brahmanical orthodoxy (the prescriptions of the priestly brahmin caste) as inadequate to their spiritual concerns. The Vedic religion that they challenged was centered on a set of texts, the Vedas, that the brahmin priests considered supernatural in origin and authoritative. These texts enjoin performance of various rituals and sacrifices, both to uphold the cosmic order and to obtain various benefits for the person in whose name the ritual or sacrifice is carried out. But the new set of ideas associated with the notions of karma and rebirth made these older religious practices seem unsatisfying. If after I die, I shall just be born into some new life, what point is there in trying to make my present situation more comfortable? Shouldn't I be more concerned with the lives to come after this one? Indeed what exactly is the point of going on to life after life? Is that cycle to go on forever? The Vedic religion seemed satisfactory as long as people held on to conventional views of human life and human happiness. If we each have just this one life on earth (and perhaps an afterlife thereafter), then it might make sense to devote it to things like sensual pleasure, wealth and power, and the social standing of a virtuous person.[2] But with the advent of new ideas about the nature of human life, the old answers no longer seemed to work. And so the *śramaṇa*s sought a new account of human happiness and how to attain it.

Among the many *śramaṇa*s, there were some who claimed to have found a solution to the problem of human existence and offered to teach it to others. Their answers differed, but one element that most shared

---

2. While the Vedas did not teach rebirth, they were not entirely clear on the question of an afterlife. Brahmanical culture of the time also recognized three possible goals in life: sensual pleasure (*kāma*), material wealth and power (*artha*), and virtue and social repute (*dharma*). For each of these goals, there was thought to be a special science concerning methods for obtaining it, and a literature developed around each of these sciences. So the *Kāma Sūtra*, for instance, is the foundational text for the traditional science of obtaining sensual pleasure.

was that true happiness could only be found by overcoming the ignorance that blinds us to our true nature. And most agreed as well that the state that is truly ideal for us must involve liberation (*mokṣa*) from the cycle of rebirths. The *śramaṇa*s also explored a wide variety of techniques for attaining this ideal state they sought. These included various ascetic practices—performing austerities such as fasting, remaining utterly motionless for long periods, abstaining from sleep, and the like. They also included various meditational or yogic practices: learning to calm the mind and focus it in one-pointed concentration, exploring a variety of altered states of consciousness, and the like.[3]

Like other new renunciants, after abandoning his life as a householder, Gautama sought to find a suitable *śramaṇa* teacher. According to our oldest accounts, he studied with several, and mastered the theories and techniques they taught but found these inadequate. He then decided to strike out on his own. Coming across an isolated forest grove, he resolved to devote a full night of concentrated effort to solving the problem of human suffering. Employing a variety of yogic techniques, he entered into four successive stages of meditation and thereby acquired three sorts of knowledge: recollection of his own past lives, understanding of the general laws of karma, and knowledge of what would come to be called the four Nobles' truths. This knowledge signaled his enlightenment (*bodhi*), his attainment of nirvāna, or liberation from rebirth. Having thus attained his goal, he considered whether or not to teach his discovery to others. At first he is said to

---

3. While the *śramaṇa* movement may have started as a protest against Brahmanical orthodoxy, the Vedic tradition eventually responded to this challenge by developing a number of its own systems for attaining liberation or *mokṣa*. These included such philosophical schools as Sāṃkhya, Nyāya, and Advaita Vedānta. These schools are referred to as "orthodox" because they accept the authority of the Vedas. In this, they differ from Buddhism and the other "heterodox" schools (such as Jainism), which deny that the Vedas have any special authoritative status. Through these orthodox schools, the Brahmanical tradition was in effect recognizing *mokṣa* as a fourth possible goal in life, in addition to the original three of *kāma*, *artha*, and *dharma*.

have been deterred by the difficulty and subtlety of the truths he had discovered. But he eventually concluded that there were some who would be able to grasp these truths and thereby profit from his discovery. So he embarked on the career of a buddha, one who has solved the problem of human suffering through their own efforts (without reliance on the teachings of others) and imparts that knowledge to others out of compassion.

There is another, far more elaborate account of Gautama's life before his enlightenment. On that account, Gautama is a prince, his father, Śuddhodana, being a powerful and wealthy king. Gautama's conception was immaculate, and he is born not in the normal way but by emerging from his mother's side without breaking her skin or otherwise causing her pain. Immediately after birth he takes seven steps in each of the four cardinal directions; the world roars in response, and blossoms spring up under his feet. A seer tells Śuddhodana that the infant will grow up to be either a buddha or a world monarch. He will become a buddha if he sees four things in his youth: an old person, a sick person, a corpse, and a wandering renunciant. If he does not see these, he will become a world monarch. Śuddhodana resolves to make sure his firstborn son becomes a mighty king, so he has Gautama raised in a luxurious palace surrounded by only young, healthy, and attractive people. Gautama grows up in these surroundings, marries, and has a son. Yet on four successive days while out hunting, he sees each of the four sights. He then resolves to become a śramana and makes his escape from the palace at night. He spends several years with a succession of teachers, but only after striking out on his own does he succeed in attaining the goal of liberation. Upon attaining enlightenment, it is Māra, the evil god of death, who tries to persuade him not to convey his discoveries to the world. Other gods then intercede to protect him from Māra's powers and ensure that there is a buddha in the world.

This more elaborate account of Gautama's early life is the one that informs popular depictions of the Buddha in Buddhist art and literature. But this version of the story only emerges several centuries after the Buddha's death. And it clearly reflects the common process whereby the life of a sect's founder comes to be draped in legend. We know, for instance, that Gautama cannot have been a prince, nor can his father have been a king since Kapilavastu was not a monarchy in his day. Likewise, the Buddha was quite insistent on the point that he was no more than an ordinary human being. This would seem to explain why the tales of miracles surrounding his birth and enlightenment are completely absent from the earliest accounts of Gautama's life. Only much later did some of his followers, perhaps out of missionary zeal, transform the story of his early life into a hagiography. Still, there are things we can learn from these legendary accretions to his biography. Consider the tale of the four sights, for instance. Why might those who shaped the legend have chosen an old person, a sick person, a corpse, and a *śramaṇa* as the sights that would spur a pampered prince to renounce his life of luxury? Clearly because the first three signify the fact of human mortality, and the existential crisis that results from this fact, while the fourth represents the possibility of averting the crisis. This point will prove useful when we try to understand the Buddha's teachings on suffering.

1.2 First Teachings

While there is not much we know with certainty about Gautama's life before his enlightenment, we know a great deal about his career as a teacher after enlightenment. For instance, we know that he first taught his new insights when he encountered five former companion renunciants at Sārnāth, near Vārānasī.[4] We will examine the record of that encounter in more detail later, but it might be helpful to begin with an overview of the discourse. The Buddha begins by addressing the

---

4. The Buddha's teachings are referred to collectively as "the Dharma." (This use of the word is often translated as "law"; we will encounter other uses of the same Sanskrit term.) The Buddhist tradition refers to the encounter at Sārnāth as "the first turning of the wheel of the Dharma."

note of skepticism with which he was initially received by his former companions. It seems that they followed a path of extreme asceticism, but when Gautama left them and struck out on his own, he abandoned such practices. So they now suspect him of having lapsed into a dissolute life. He thus begins by describing the path he has discovered as a "middle path" between two extremes, those of asceticism and the life of sensual pleasure. He then describes this path as "the Nobles' eightfold path,"[5] listing its eight component practices: right view, right intention, right speech, right action, right livelihood, right exertion, right self-possession, and right concentration. This leads naturally to the enumeration of the four Nobles' truths since the claim that there is such a path is the fourth of the four truths. The four are, in summary form:

1. There is suffering.

2. There is the origination of suffering: suffering comes into existence in dependence on causes.

3. There is the cessation of suffering: all future suffering can be prevented.

4. There is a path to the cessation of suffering.

The second truth is later elaborated in terms of a twelve-linked chain of causes and effects, the first of which is ignorance. And the ignorance in question will be explained as failure to know three characteristics of reality: impermanence, suffering, and non-self. It is thus significant that the Buddha goes on to teach the five renunciants the doctrine that there is no self, and moreover that he argues for non-self on the grounds that all the constituents of the person are impermanent. Finally, according to the sūtra that recounts this first teaching, it ended with all five śramaṇas attaining enlightenment, so that there were then six people in the state of nirvāna.

---

5. This is more commonly translated as "the noble eightfold path." But the word corresponding to "noble" here (*ārya*) refers to those who have attained enlightenment. So the eightfold path is the one followed by the Nobles.

To summarize, in this early episode in the Buddha's teaching career, we find reference to the following doctrines and ideas:

the Dharma as a middle path

the eightfold path

the four Nobles' truths

twelve-linked chain of dependent origination

three characteristics of existence

Let us now look at these in somewhat more detail. The doctrine of the four truths plays a central organizing function in the Buddha's teachings, so we should begin there. The first of these, that there is suffering, seems clear enough. And it would be hard to deny that it is true; there is all too much suffering in the world. But this then raises the question of why the Buddha should have thought it necessary to point it out. In fact, Buddhists claim this truth, properly understood, is among the hardest for most people to acknowledge. This is the first of the four truths because the Buddha thinks it is something about which ordinary people are all in denial. To see why he thinks this, we need to understand just what is meant here by "suffering." And here is where the legend of the four sights becomes relevant. What it tells us is that by this term, Buddhists do not mean ordinary pain, such as what we feel when we are injured or sick. Instead, they mean existential suffering— the frustration, alienation, and despair that result from the realization of our own mortality. Remember that according to the legend, Gautama would not have become a buddha had he not encountered the facts of old age, disease, decay, and death until late in his life. What is it about these facts that make their recognition significant? Well, we each want our own lives to go well. We want to be happy. And when we want happiness, what we want requires a sense that our lives have meaning, value, and purpose. Of course, different individuals are made happy by different sorts of things. But when something makes someone happy, that's because they take it as saying good things about who they are and where they are going. The difficulty is that once we are forced to acknowledge our own mortality, it becomes difficult to sustain the sense that events can have significance for our lives. How can anything contribute to the meaning of my life when in the long run, I shall be dead, with the world going merrily on its way without me? Now we all know at some level that someday we will die, yet we still seem to live our lives on the assumption that death can be indefinitely postponed. It is when events show this assumption to be false that existential suffering arises.

Here is one point at which you might think it makes a difference whether or not we accept the doctrine of karma and rebirth. Indeed, you might think that the account of existential suffering that has just been given only makes sense if we deny this doctrine. And since the Buddhists accept the doctrine, you might suspect that they must mean something else by "suffering" than existential suffering, the sense of alienation and despair that comes from recognizing the implications of our own mortality. After all, if we live another life after we die, my death can't be the end of me. And if what I do in this life determines what sort of life I get next time around, wouldn't what happens to me now always have meaning for my future existence? So why would existential suffering arise for someone who accepted karma and rebirth? The Buddhist will reply, though, that these suspicions merely illustrate how difficult it can be to grasp the true nature of suffering. The tradition distinguishes among three different layers within the notion of suffering, each more subtle than the preceding: suffering due to pain, suffering due to impermanence, and suffering due to conditions. It is the last of these that is meant to explain why the fact of rebirth itself constitutes a kind of existential suffering. But to see why they think this, we need to say something about the first two ways in which they claim we experience suffering.

The first includes all those experiences that we would ordinarily classify as painful: being cut, burnt, or struck; having a toothache or headache; losing a prized possession; not getting the job we'd set our hearts on; and the like. Note that even with such simple cases as a toothache, there are actually two levels to the negative nature of the experience. First, there is the feeling of pain itself, the immediate sensation of hurting. But there is also the worry that we commonly experience when we have something like a toothache: What does this painful feeling say about who I am and where I am going? Even when we don't put it to ourselves in so many words, this sense of "dis-ease,"[6] of not being at home with ourselves, can permeate our lives when we have some nagging pain, undermining even our enjoyment of ordinary pleasures.

The second form of suffering includes all negative experiences deriving from impermanence. This has a much wider scope than one might suspect. As we will later see in more detail, Buddhists claim that everything that originates in dependence on causes must also cease to exist. And since all those things we ordinarily care about are dependent on causes, it follows that they are all impermanent. Now the pain of a toothache could be counted among the experiences that derive from impermanence: we get toothaches because healthy teeth are impermanent. But it is not just getting something we don't want, like a toothache, that is included here. Getting something we do want also comes under the category of suffering as impermanence. It probably seems counterintuitive to classify getting what you desire—a car, a job, a child, the esteem of people you care about, happiness for a friend—as a negative experience. But this is why Buddhists call this kind of suffering more subtle than the first. There is suffering in getting what one wants because the desired object is impermanent. So the happiness we feel is always tinged with anxiety about losing it. Indeed the feeling of happiness we derive from getting what we want is itself impermanent. When the novelty wears off, so does the feeling of happiness, which is why we seem to always be in pursuit of something

---

6. "Dis-ease" might be a better translation of the Sanskrit term we are discussing here, *duḥkha*, than "suffering." This term is formed from the prefix *duḥ*, which is related to the English "dis," plus the noun *kha*, which originally meant a hole or space, but came to mean "happiness," or "ease."

new. This explains the pattern we follow: always formulating some new goal, some new object of desire, when we get what we previously wanted (or give it up as unattainable). And when we begin to notice this pattern in our behavior, the happiness we feel on obtaining something new begins to drain away.

The last point leads naturally to the third level of suffering, suffering due to conditions. By "conditions," here is meant the factors that are said to be responsible for rebirth (namely, the intentions or volitions that motivate actions and cause karmic fruit). So suffering due to conditions refers to the suffering that results from rebirth. But to revert to the question we asked earlier, why should the mere fact of rebirth count as a form of suffering? Some specific rebirths might be quite unpleasant. But if we knew the karmic causal laws, we might be able to avoid those and obtain only rebirths in relatively fortunate circumstances. Why would that still count as suffering? The answer is encapsulated in the fact that re-birth also entails re-death. When we think that rebirth would help us avoid the suffering that is due to our own impermanence (i.e., our mortality), we are forgetting that rebirth means re-encountering that very impermanence we wish to escape. Once we take this into account, the prospect no longer seems quite so inviting. Indeed the idea of perpetually going through this cycle—being born, living a life, losing that life, and then starting anew—can only inspire a kind of cosmic ennui: What could possibly be the point? What we are now faced with is the requirement that there be an endless succession of future lives in order to sustain the sense that the life I am now living has a point. But if this life gets its point from the next, and that from its successor, and so on, will this really work? Perhaps the doctrine of karma and rebirth, instead of undercutting the claim that sentient beings are subject to suffering, actually reinforces the point.

It might be natural at this point to wonder if the Buddha was not unduly pessimistic. Surely life is not all doom and gloom. And perhaps with a little luck and some good sense, one can live a life that is predominantly characterized by happiness. Of course, the Buddhist will respond that this is just what nirvāna amounts to. But the opponent will say that seeking nirvāna seems a rather drastic step. For this requires abandoning much of what is usually thought to give life value, the pursuit of the three (worldly) goals: sensual pleasure, wealth and power, and virtue and repute. Surely at least some people can live lives that are happily devoted to such conventional ends as family, career, and recreation. The Buddhist will respond that such pursuits can sometimes give pleasure and happiness. Buddhists do not deny that people sometimes experience pleasure and happiness. They claim, though, that pleasure and happiness are deceptive in nature: being in these states leads us to believe that they can be made to endure, when in fact, for the reasons sketched above, they cannot. And in the long run, they claim, those reasons dictate that the happiness one obtains from such pursuits will be outweighed by the suffering. The pursuit of happiness will become a kind of treadmill, and the sense that we are on this treadmill leads to alienation and despair. For anyone who is at all reflective about their life, it is inevitable that the happiness in their life will be outweighed by the suffering.

Here is one last question before we move on: Might antidepressants help? Modern medicine has developed a class of drugs designed to help people who have lost all sense of enjoyment in their lives. And the more subtle sense of suffering that we have just been discussing sounds somewhat like this condition. Could a simple pill be an alternative to the arduous task of seeking enlightenment? Here is one possible way the Buddhist might respond to this question. First, they might claim that no pill can alter the facts. Taking a pill might alter how we assess those facts, but that is another matter entirely. For what the pill might actually do is foster an illusion, creating the sense that we can continue to ignore those facts. Suppose that by taking an antidepressant, we could avoid the sense that the happiness-seeking project is an endless treadmill. We might then be looking at the same facts that led the Buddha to his analysis of suffering, but we would be seeing those facts in a different light. The Buddhist would claim, though, that our assessment of the facts would be unrealistic. Taking the pill would simply re-instill the illusion that conventional happiness is attainable in the long run. And this, they would hold, is no alternative to facing the facts squarely and taking the appropriate action—seeking nirvāna.[7] So now let's sharpen the question. Assume that by taking a pill one could permanently prevent the subtle sense of suffering from arising. Assume as well that the Buddha's analysis is correct, that the happiness-seeking project really is an endless treadmill. Would it actually be better to not take the pill, face up to the facts, and seek nirvāna? The Buddhist seems to assume it would be, but why? What assumption would their answer seem to be based on? And do you think that assumption is correct?

1.3 The Cause and Cure of Suffering

While the first of the four Nobles' truths points out the existence of suffering, the second—that suffering depends on causes—is meant to explain how it originates. The underlying idea at work here is that by learning the cause of some phenomenon, we may become able to exercise control over it. So the Buddha gives a detailed account of the factors he claims are the conditions in dependence on which suffering arises. This account, the twelve-linked chain of dependent origination, is traditionally understood as describing a sequence that takes place over three successive lives. In one life, there occurs (1) ignorance (namely ignorance of the fact that all sentient existence is characterized by impermanence, suffering, and non-self), and because of its occurrence, there occur (2) volitions (*samskāras*), understood as the active forces in

---

7. This is not to deny that antidepressants can be genuinely helpful for those suffering from clinical depression. The Buddhist claims that the happiness-seeking project cannot be sustained in the long run. While this might seem like a depressing analysis, remember that they also claim there is a better alternative to that project, namely nirvāna. And they think we should make the effort to seek that better alternative. Someone who is clinically depressed might not be capable of making such an effort. Their sense of the futility of it all might render them unable to do anything to better their situation. A Buddhist might then say that antidepressants would be useful in their case.

karma. It is in dependence on these volitions in the one life that there occurs (3) consciousness in the next life. That is, rebirth (in the form of the first moment of consciousness in a new life) occurs because of the desires that led to the performance of actions in the past life. On this consciousness, in turn, depends the occurrence of (4) a sentient body. That is, it is due to that first moment of rebirth consciousness that the organized matter of the fetal body comes to be a sentient being. On the existence of the sentient body, in turn, depend (5) the six sense faculties (the five external senses plus an "inner sense" that is sensitive to internal states such as pain). On these depend (6) contact or sensory stimulation. And given sensory stimulation, there arises (7) feeling, i.e., the hedonic states of pleasure, pain, and indifference. Feeling, in turn, causes (8) desire, and desire leads to (9) appropriation (upādāna), the attitude whereby one takes certain things as being "me" or "mine." In dependence on appropriation, there originates (10) becoming. This is explained as consisting of the volitions that bring about the next rebirth, as well as the psychophysical elements making up the sentient body in that rebirth. In dependence on this, there is (11) birth, i.e., rebirth into the third life. And in dependence on birth, there is (12) old age and death, here taken as indicating all existential suffering.

There are obviously some difficulties in this list. For instance, the tenth condition, becoming, seems to involve a repetition of the second, volition, and the fourth, sentient body. It also seems odd that birth into the third life should be listed as a separate condition, while birth into the second life is not. There is another version of the list that omits the six sense faculties and instead has the sentient body serve as the condition for consciousness. Since consciousness has already been said to be the condition for sentient body, this has the effect of making consciousness both the cause and the effect of sentient body.[8] And there

8. It is this version of the list that will later lead some Abhidharma philosophers to hold that two simultaneously existing things can be both cause and effect of one another. This notion of simultaneous reciprocal causation became the subject of an Abhidharma controversy.

are versions of the list with only ten links, omitting the first two conditions altogether. These and other problems have led some scholars
to suggest that our list of twelve results from the fusion of what were
originally two or more separate lists.

But let us put such questions to one side and look instead at the
basic logic underlying the list that we have. The idea seems to be this.
One is born into this life because in the last life, one acted on the
basis of volitions that were formed in ignorance of the facts about
our existence. Having been born with a body, senses, and mind, one
comes in contact with sense objects, and this cognitive contact brings
about feelings of pleasure, pain, and indifference. These feelings trig-
ger desires, and desires that are conditioned by ignorance lead to the
stance known as appropriation: taking certain things (including things
that no longer exist or do not yet exist) as "me," and other things as
"mine" or my possessions. It is this stance that fuels rebirth, and this
produces the suffering that is associated with all sentient existence.

How, one might wonder, could the first condition, ignorance,
occur without there already being a sentient being (something that is
not found until the fourth link in the series)? Doesn't ignorance require
someone whose ignorance it is? When we wonder this, we are taking
this list as an account of the very beginning of the series of lives. But
the commentators tell us that the list should not be taken this way.
What is here treated as the first life in a sequence of three is itself the
effect of prior conditions that occurred in some yet earlier life.[9] So it is

---

9. The Buddha says in this connection that we cannot discern the very first
life in the series of lives we have lived. In the later tradition, this is often taken
to mean that the series of lives (and so our ignorance as well) is beginningless.
But the Buddha's statement might be interpreted another way: while there
might have been a very first life in the series, we could never tell which one
that is. For it's always possible that although there were earlier lives, we simply
can't remember any. Given this difficulty, it is pointless to speculate about
whether there is or is not a first life in the series and what might explain this.
Suffering exists in the present life, and such speculation won't help solve that
problem.

not saying that ignorance occurred before there were mind and body. Ignorance comes first on the list because of its key role in producing suffering. In effect, what we have in this theory is an account of how ignorance, by bringing about suffering, reinforces and thus perpetuates itself. (We'll discuss how it plays this role when we come to the three characteristics.) When the chain of dependent origination is seen in this way, it is even possible to separate it from the doctrine of karma and rebirth. What it then amounts to is basically just the claim that the ignorance occurring at any one point in one's life causes one to act in certain ways that set the stage for both later suffering and continued ignorance.

The third truth, that there is the cessation of suffering, follows directly from the second truth. Ignorance is a remediable condition. Since it is possible to cure our ignorance, it is possible to put an end to the feedback loop that results in suffering. The fourth truth then spells out a set of eight practices that are designed to bring about this cure. They are, once again: right view, right intention, right speech, right action, right livelihood, right exertion, right self-possession, and right concentration. These eight are said to fall into three basic kinds: the first two represent wisdom, the next three are the factors of morality, and the final three are the practices that make up meditation. The factors are listed in a way that might suggest a sequential order: start with right view, follow the rules of right conduct, proceed to concentration, and then attain nirvāna. But in actual practice, the different factors are said to mutually reinforce one another so that the mastery of each will involve contributions from the others. For instance, one might begin by acquiring a rudimentary grasp of the basic teachings of the Buddha (right view), on that basis form the (right) intention to seek nirvāna, and then set about trying to obey the moral rules set out for lay followers, such as not lying (right speech), not stealing (right action), and not working as a butcher (right livelihood). But when following these moral rules becomes habitual, this has the effect of clearing the mind of certain passions that can interfere with attaining wisdom. So this can lead to a deeper appreciation of the Buddha's teachings (right view), followed by the (right) intention to become a monk or nun. Entrance into the order of Buddhist monks and nuns (the *saṃgha*) brings with it a new set of moral virtues one must acquire. Practice in accordance with these virtues, along with the newly deepened understanding of the Dharma, helps one then begin to engage in meditation. But meditating also makes it easier to attain the required moral virtues. And meditation likewise produces insights into the nature of the mind that further strengthen one's appreciation of the Dharma. And so on.

For our purposes, the reciprocal relation between wisdom and meditation is particularly significant. In the context of the Buddhist path, "wisdom" means the practice of philosophy—analyzing concepts, investigating arguments, considering objections, and the like. So the content of this "wisdom" is just the Buddhist philosophy that we are examining here. Now we already know that Buddhists claim ignorance is ultimately responsible for our suffering. And wisdom looks like the antidote to ignorance. So it makes sense that Buddhism should claim doing philosophy is necessary for attaining enlightenment. But will doing philosophy be sufficient? Buddhists generally say no. And it's not too difficult to guess why this is. For we also know something about what this ignorance supposedly consists in: the failure to recognize the three characteristics, the facts of impermanence, suffering, and non-self. This failure is exhibited in some fundamental assumptions we make about our lives: that we and the things we want can continue to exist indefinitely, that we can attain happiness by pursuing conventional goals, and that there is a true "me" for whom this life can have meaning and value. Since almost everything we do is based on these assumptions, we are constantly in the business of reinforcing them. So even if our philosophical practice tells us they are false, it may not be so easy to uproot them. The situation here is like the case of a smoker. They may know perfectly well that smoking shortens their life. But each cigarette smoked reinforces their addiction, making it harder to act on that knowledge. So, the Buddhist says, meditation is needed in order to break the cycle and bring home the knowledge gained through philosophy.

To learn to meditate is to learn to control the mind. That control is then used to examine various mental processes, and to counteract those processes that perpetuate ignorance and suffering. So through meditation, one can supposedly confirm that there is no self, by observing how impermanent mental states actually do all the work that we imagine could only be done by an enduring self. We can also see how certain mental states, such as anger and hatred, can reinforce belief in a self and thus perpetuate ignorance. And through meditation, we can then learn to counteract such states. In the case of anger and hatred, for instance, the adept is taught to cultivate feelings of kindness and sympathetic joy toward ever-larger circles of beings, starting with friends and loved ones and eventually extending to those toward whom they feel anger and enmity. So meditation serves as a necessary supplement to philosophy in Buddhist practice. (This is why, even if the Buddhist philosophers are right about things, studying Buddhist philosophy wouldn't bring about liberation by itself.)

At the same time, doing philosophy is said to be necessary if the practice of meditation is to be effective. For one thing, many meditational attainments involve altered states of consciousness. What one is aware of in these states is very different from what goes on in our ordinary experience. This means that we need a conceptual framework to help us sort out our experiences in meditation and figure out what their significance is. Otherwise, we would be confronted with what could only seem like a buzzing, whirring mass of confusion. Doing philosophy is said to help us acquire the conceptual tools that help us understand what we encounter in meditation. So for instance, mastery of the philosophical arguments for the non-existence of a self will make it easier to appreciate the significance of the complex causal connections we find when we closely observe what superficially seem like simple mental processes. That there are these causal connections will then be seen to confirm that there is no self standing behind the scenes directing our mental processes. And this will bring home the truth of non-self as it applies to our own case. So while meditation is meant to help the practitioner apply the knowledge they acquire through philosophy, philosophy, in turn, plays an important role in facilitating meditational practice.

Just as there are interesting relationships among the components of the eightfold path, so it is worthwhile to examine how the three characteristics are related to one another. Suffering is caused, we are told, by ignorance of impermanence, suffering, and non-self. And it is overcome by coming to fully know these three facts about the world. We now have some understanding of what Buddhists mean by the truth of suffering. Suppose they are right in their claims about what suffering is and why it arises in lives lived in the ordinary way. They also claim that everything is impermanent and that sentient beings are devoid of selves. Suppose these claims are also true. What might they have to do with the claim about suffering? It is tempting to think that impermanence is the chief factor here. On this interpretation, it is the fact that everything is impermanent that makes it true both that suffering is inevitable and that there is no self. On this account, we wrongly believe that the things we desire are permanent, we become attached to them, and then we suffer when they reveal their impermanence by going out of existence. Likewise, we base our lives on the assumption that we have permanent selves and then suffer when our mortality shows this assumption to be false. The solution is then to learn to live with the fact of impermanence. Suffering will cease when we stop clinging to things and learn to live in the moment.

While this interpretation of the three characteristics is tempting, it is wrong. It is the truth of non-self that is said to be key to understanding suffering's genesis and dissolution. And the interpretation just offered does not take sufficiently seriously the fact of non-self. For what it assumes is that I do have a self, just a very impermanent one. This is the assumption behind the advice that we live our lives in the present moment. This advice would make sense only if there were a true "me" that could derive value and significance from its experiences, but that existed only for a short while, to be replaced by a new self, someone who is not "me" but someone else. We are being advised to live in the present precisely because when we plan for the future instead, we are letting the interests of that future self dictate what this present self does. Now, while Buddhism is sometimes understood in this way, this is clearly incompatible with the claim that there is no self. Indeed this turns out to be one of the extreme views that the Dharma is supposed to be a middle path between.[10] So this cannot be how to understand the three characteristics.

The doctrine of non-self is widely acknowledged to be the most difficult to grasp of all the basic teachings of Buddhism. The whole of the next chapter will be devoted to examining its intricacies. But for now we can perhaps say this much about it and its relation to the other two of the three characteristics. Recall that by "suffering" what Buddhists mean first and foremost is existential suffering. And existential suffering derives from the assumption that there is a "me" to serve as a potential bearer of value and significance. Such suffering arises out of the suspicion that the kind of meaning and value we want is not to be had— that our best efforts at attaining happiness will inevitably be frustrated. And we experience suffering precisely because this seems like such an affront to the dignity of the being we take ourselves to be. Now suppose it could be shown that while there are the experiences that make up a lifetime, those experiences have no owner. There is no "me," no experiencer whose experiences they are. In that case, the conviction that my life should have uniquely special value and significance to me would

---

10. This is what is called "annihilationism," the view that while I exist now, when the parts that presently make me up cease to exist, I will go utterly out of existence, typically to be replaced by someone else. The other member of the pair, in this case, is called "eternalism." It is the view that the true "me" is eternal. The theory of dependent origination is said to constitute a middle path between these two extremes. We will have more to say about all this in the next chapter.

turn out to be based on a mistake. For experiences in my life to have meaning, there must be more than just the experiences; there must be something separate from them for which they have good or bad meanings. Without belief in a separate self, existential suffering would no longer arise. Such suffering requires belief in something whose demand for meaning and significance is violated. It requires belief in a self. Impermanence also plays a role here. It is the fact of impermanence that first awakens us to suffering. And the fact that (almost) everything is impermanent will play a major role in the arguments for non-self. But it is non-self that plays the central role. And it is our false belief in a self that Buddhists identify as the core of our ignorance.

1.4 Living without Suffering

What might it be like to be enlightened? The Buddha claims that at the end of his path lies the cessation of suffering. And we've just looked at how following the path might bring that about. But even if we can make some sort of sense of his path as a cure for suffering, this only tells us what being enlightened is not like. Being enlightened would mean being without existential suffering. Is there anything positive to be said about it? Is it pleasant? Is the enlightened person happy? Or is it just that because it's devoid of suffering, it's the best we can hope for? This would be a reasonable question to ask for someone considering whether or not to follow the Buddha's advice. The "live for the moment" idea that was just rejected as an interpretation of the three characteristics did have the advantage that it implied an answer to this question. For then, the enlightened person would appreciate their present experiences without any concern about what is to come in the future. And perhaps this would enhance the enjoyment of any good experiences while diminishing the anxiety that normally accompanies bad experiences. So perhaps on that interpretation being enlightened would be pleasant. But since that is not what Buddhist enlightenment is like, it does not answer our question.

Here is another place where the doctrine of karma and rebirth has a role to play. To become enlightened is to enter into the state of nirvāna. The Sanskrit term *nirvāna* literally means "extinction" or "going out" (as when a fire is said to go out). What gets extinguished is, of course, suffering. But it sometimes seems as if Buddhists equate this extinction with another sort of extinction, namely the end of the series of rebirths. What would that be like? Well, if there is no self, then to say I won't be reborn is to say I will cease to exist. Is this what nirvāna is, utter and complete annihilation? If so, then our question is answered in the negative: enlightenment would have no positive result, only the purely negative one of escape from all further suffering. And since this escape looks like a state of pure non-being, an utter blank, it also seems singularly unappealing.

That there is something wrong with this understanding of nir-vāna is suggested by the fact that one of the extreme views the Buddha rejects is called "annihilationism." Moreover, when the Buddha is asked about the fate of the enlightened person after death, he says it would not be correct to say they are utterly non-existent. But the explication of these claims will have to wait until Chapter 3, §1. What we can say at this point is that there is more to nirvāna than what happens after the death of an enlightened person. There is also the state of the person between the time of attaining enlightenment and the time of death. In discussing the goal of their practice, Buddhists draw a distinction between "cessation with remainder" and "cessation without remainder." By "cessation" is meant stopping the accumulation of new karma, which happens at the time of enlightenment. And the "remainder" is the residual karma that keeps the present life going. Once that residue is exhausted, this life ends. So they distinguish between nirvāna as the state of a living enlightened person, and nirvāna as the state of the enlightened person after death.[11] If we want

---

11. This is sometimes referred to as *parinirvāna*, though strictly speaking that term only applies to the death of a buddha.

to know if there is anything positive to the state of nirvāna, the place to look would seem to be this cessation with remainder.

Unfortunately, there isn't much in the early Buddhist texts about this state. There is a great deal about how to attain cessation, but not much about what it is like to have attained it and remain alive. Artistic depictions of the Buddha and other enlightened persons often portray them with a serene half-smile on their faces, and this would seem to suggest that there is a kind of quiet happiness to the state. But this is not stated explicitly in our sources. Buddhists were not, though, the only Indian philosophers to teach the goal of liberation from rebirth. And among the other Indian philosophers who discuss liberation, some also draw a distinction between the state of postmortem liberation (*mukti*) and the state of being liberated but still alive (*jīvan-mukti*). In addition, there is also a debate among the orthodox schools as to whether liberation is pleasant or joyful. Now the latter debate concerns the postmortem state. It is possible for these schools to have such a debate because they all affirm the existence of a self. So unlike the Buddhists, they all claim that the liberated person continues to exist when their last life is over. Some, though, claim that the self enjoys eternal bliss in this state of postmortem liberation, while others deny this. Indeed some of the latter go so far as to say that the self feels nothing in this state, that its existence forever after is indistinguishable from that of a rock. Moreover, those who deny that the liberated self enjoys happiness after death also do not, as a rule, acknowledge a special state of liberation while still alive.

Now all the (non-Buddhist) parties to this debate agree that liberation is the supreme goal for humans. They also agree that ignorance about who we truly are is what keeps us in the unliberated state—by making us pursue inappropriate goals like sensual pleasure, wealth and power, and virtue and repute. Since they all seem to mean more or less the same thing by liberation, this makes us wonder why some would deny that the supremely valuable end has any intrinsically desirable features. Why would they expect anyone to seek a state whose only attraction lies in the absence of pain and suffering? If that were all that was being offered, wouldn't most people figure they could beat the odds and stick with the strategy of seeking ordinary happiness?

This is not a question we can definitively answer by examining the texts of these orthodox schools. But a bit of speculation might throw some light on the situation here, and in so doing suggest an answer to our question about Buddhist nirvāna. Suppose that, as the Bhagavad Gītā says, "desire is here the enemy" (BG III.37). That is, what keeps us bound to the wheel of *saṃsāra* (the state of perpetual rebirth and its suffering) is our desire for things like sensual pleasure, wealth and power, and virtue and repute. Desire for these things is problematic because it is based on the false assumption that I am something that could be made better off by having them. Further, suppose that were it not for such desires, and the ignorance about our identity that they both presuppose and reinforce, we would be in a state that is intrinsically valuable. Suppose, that is, that to be liberated from saṃsāra is to enjoy true happiness, perhaps even true bliss. There then arises what we could call the paradox of liberation. This paradox involves the following propositions, each of which seems true to the orthodox Indian philosophers:

1. Liberation is inherently desirable.

2. Selfish desires prevent one from attaining liberation.

3. In order to attain liberation one must train oneself to live without selfish desires.

4. One does not engage in deliberate action unless one desires the foreseen result of the action.

Taken together, propositions (3) and (4) tell us that no one will set about trying to attain liberation unless they desire it. And proposition (2) tells us that no one will attain liberation unless they seek it. Liberation isn't something people just fall into through dumb luck. You have to make an effort to overcome ignorance; otherwise, it will just perpetuate your bondage in saṃsāra. Putting these things together, we get the result that you have to desire liberation to obtain it. And (1) tells us that it's reasonable to desire liberation. The trouble is (2) also tells us that if we desire liberation, we won't get it. So although it's reasonable to want liberation, it's impossible to get it, so it isn't reasonable to want it after all. This is a paradox.

There are different strategies we might use to try to resolve the paradox of liberation. We might deny (1), though that would then raise the question of why anyone should be interested in attaining liberation. Or we might claim that the desire for liberation is not a selfish desire. But this seems implausible if (1) is true. If liberation is such a good thing, then surely my wanting to attain it would count as a selfish desire—a desire to benefit myself. Perhaps, though, not all such desires are selfish in the sense that's relevant for (2) to apply. Remember that the trouble with desires is supposed to be that they reinforce the wrong view about who we really are. What if liberation were joyful in a way that didn't conflict with the facts about who we really are? The difficulty is that even if this were true, those of us who have not experienced this bliss would have trouble thinking of it in anything other than conventional terms. When told that liberation is a state of bliss, we would imagine it to be like intense sensual pleasure or the thrill that can come from gaining great wealth and power. We would then end up desiring liberation in just the wrong way—the way that (2) says prevents our attaining it. But this suggests a possible strategy: deny (1) not because it is false but because it is misleading for those with conventional views about what is desirable. For this audience, what should be emphasized is not what is positively good about liberation, but rather that to be liberated is to be forever free of pain and suffering. Then they might attain the bliss of liberation without having aimed at it. Their desire would just have been to rid themselves of pain and suffering.

There are situations where this sort of indirect strategy is known to work. Consider the "warm and fuzzy" feeling we get when we act benevolently, doing something good for someone else. We get this feeling of gratification when our aim is to help others instead of ourselves. But this means that if the only reason I ever helped others were because I wanted to have this warm and fuzzy feeling, I would never succeed. If my helping someone else were part of a calculated strategy whose ultimate purpose was to benefit myself, I wouldn't get the warm and fuzzy feeling at all. I can't get the feeling by aiming at it. I only get the feeling when I aim at something else—benefitting another person. Does this mean there is a paradox of benevolence? No, we can and do sometimes act benevolently, and thereby get the warm and fuzzy feeling. The best advice to give someone who wants to feel good in this way is that they should become genuinely concerned about the welfare of others. And this is something we can learn to do. We can get the warm and fuzzy feeling indirectly—not by aiming at it but by aiming at something else. There is no paradox of benevolence.

Could something like this be what's going on in the case of those orthodox Indian schools that deny liberation is pleasant or happy? Perhaps they are simply tailoring their advice to their understanding of their audience's present state of mind. Perhaps because their audience would misunderstand the happiness that comes with liberation and then want it in a way that would prevent them from ever getting it, these schools advise their audience to aim at something else, the cessation of suffering. And perhaps we should understand what Early Buddhism says about nirvāna in a similar way. On this interpretation, the fact that nirvāna is depicted primarily negatively, as just the permanent cessation of suffering, and the fact that very little positive is ever said about cessation with remainder, represent strategic choices. They do not necessarily reflect the nature of nirvāna. Perhaps cessation with remainder is a state of true happiness, though this is importantly different from what is ordinarily taken for happiness.

Something like this interpretation may be necessary if the Buddha's path is going to make sense to those who don't accept the doctrine of karma and rebirth. If there is no rebirth, but the Buddha is right that there is no self, then after I die, there won't be any suffering regardless of whether or not I attain enlightenment. So telling me that cessation without remainder is devoid of suffering won't motivate me to try to attain enlightenment. I'll only be motivated by facts about cessation with remainder, the state of being enlightened but still alive. And it isn't clear that being told this state is devoid of all existential suffering would be enough. If that were all I thought I'd get out of enlightenment, I might calculate the odds and decide that I'd do better to pursue conventional happiness. It might be that only a positive portrayal of enlightenment as true happiness would motivate me to seek it. And then there is the question of whether my desire for enlightenment would get in the way of my ever attaining it. But this is a question to which we will have to return. For we have not yet considered what it might be like to come to believe that we do not have selves. And coming to believe this is an important component of being enlightened. The Buddhist doctrine of non-self will be the subject of our next chapter. Then in Chapter 3, we will come back to this question of what it might be like to be enlightened.

Some Key Points of This Chapter

- A basic framework of the Buddha's teachings is the four Nobles' truths: that there is suffering, that suffering is caused, that there is nirvāna or the extinguishing of suffering, and that there is a path to the extinguishing of suffering.

- The suffering that the Buddhist path is meant to extinguish is existential suffering.

- According to the teaching of dependent origination, the ultimate cause of suffering is ignorance of the fact that all sentient existence is characterized by suffering, impermanence, and non-self.

- The path to the cessation of suffering taught by the Buddha involves practices—including both meditation and the cultivation of philosophical wisdom—designed to undermine our sense of a self.

• While Buddhism is relatively silent on whether the state of nirvāna, the life of an enlightened person, is positively good, this might be just to prevent the unenlightened from desiring it in a way that reinforces belief in a self.

For Further Reading

For more on the details of the Buddha's life and teaching career see Chapters 3 and 4 of A. K. Warder, *Indian Buddhism* (Delhi: Motilal Banarsidass, 1970).

For discussion of the controversy among scholars concerning whether there was a historical Buddha, see Oskar von Hinüber, "The Buddha as a Historical Person," *Journal of the International Association of Buddhist Studies* 42 (2019): 231–64.

The account of the Buddha's first expounding of his path (S IV.420–4) may be found at Bhikkhu Bodhi, trans., *The Connected Discourses of the Buddha* (Boston: Wisdom Publications, 2000), pp. 1843–47.

For a more detailed account of the reciprocal relationships among the different parts of the eightfold path, see David Burton, *Buddhism, Knowledge and Liberation* (Aldershot, UK: Ashgate, 2004), pp. 62–75.

For a discussion of the debate among Hindu schools concerning whether liberation is desirable, see Arindam Chakrabarti, "Is Liberation (*Mokṣa*) Pleasant?" *Philosophy East and West* 33, no. 2 (April 1983): pp. 167–82.

The alleged paradox of benevolence, and its resolution, were formulated by the eighteenth century British philosopher and theologian Joseph Butler. For discussion see Amélie Oksenberg Rorty, "Butler on Benevolence and Conscience," *Philosophy* 53, no. 204 (1978): 171–84.

Chapter Two

Empty Persons

The Buddha holds that we experience the suffering of saṃsāra because of our ignorance of the three characteristics: impermanence, suffering, and non-self. Of these three, it is the characteristic of non-self that plays the central role in his diagnosis. According to Early Buddhism, there is no self, and persons are not ultimately real. This may be put somewhat cryptically as: we are empty persons, persons who are empty of selves. In this chapter, we will investigate this claim. We will look at some of the arguments found in early Buddhist texts for the claim that there is no self. And we shall try to determine what it means to say that persons are not ultimately real. But before we can do either of these things, we need to determine what it would mean to say that there is a self. The word "self" gets used in several different ways, only one of which is relevant to the philosophical question the Buddha is trying to answer. We can avoid much confusion about what Buddhists mean by their doctrine of non-self if we begin by getting clear concerning what they have in mind when they speak of a self.

2.1 Self As Essence

By "the self," what Buddhists mean is the essence of a person—the one part whose continued existence is required for that person to continue to exist. This is the definition of "self" that we will be working with. But what does it mean? It might be helpful to think of the view that there is a self as one possible answer to the question of what the word "I" refers to. I am a person. And persons are made up of a variety of constituents: parts making up the body, such as limbs and organs, and parts making up the mind, such as thoughts, feelings, and desires.

Now persons are things that continue to exist for some time—at least a lifetime, if not longer. But not all the parts of a person must continue to exist in order for that person to continue to exist. I could survive the loss of a finger or toe. And I might lose my desire for coffee without ceasing to exist. So apparently, not all the parts of a person are necessary to the continued existence of a person. To say there is a self is to say that there is some one part that is necessary. This one part would then be what the word "I" really named. The other parts would more properly be called "mine"; only that one essential part would count as the true "me." The alternative to this would be to say that "I" refers to all the parts collectively. Let us call this alternative the view that "I" is the name of the person, where by "person" we mean the whole that consists of all the parts that make up my body and mind over the duration of my existence. So either "I" is the name of one essential part of the person or else it refers to the person as a whole. (Of course, this applies to the other words we use to refer to persons as well, such as names as well as other personal pronouns.)

To say there is a self is to say that there is one part of the person that accounts for the identity of that person over time. If there were a self, then the person whose self it was would continue to exist as long as that part continued to exist. The self would then be the basis of a person's identity over time. It would be what explained why this present person, me, is the same person as some earlier person. But we need to be careful with the expression "same person." For the English word "same" is ambiguous. When we say "x and y are the same," there are two things we might mean. We could mean that x and y are qualitatively identical, or we could mean that x and y are numerically identical. To say that x and y are qualitatively identical is to say that they share the same qualities, that they resemble one another or are alike. To say that x and y are numerically identical is to say that they are one and the same thing, that x and y are really just two names for one entity. So there can be cases of qualitative identity but numerical distinctness, as with two T-shirts that come out of the factory looking exactly alike. And there can also be cases of numerical identity but qualitative distinctness, as with a leaf that in summer is green and smooth but in autumn is red and crinkled. We said above that according to the self-theorist, a self is what explains why some person existing now is the same person as someone who existed earlier. The key thing to keep in mind is that here "same" is meant in the sense of numerical identity.[1]

Like many other things, persons can undergo very significant qualitative changes and yet continue to exist. I can continue to exist as one and the same person, me, even though the properties I now have are quite different from those I used to have. Thanks to the ambiguity of the English word "same," we can put this as, "He is the same person but not the same." When we say this, we are not contradicting ourselves. The first "same" ("the same person") is used in the sense of numerical identity. The second "same" is used in the sense of qualitative identity; "not the same" means qualitatively distinct. It is one person, me, who once had the property of liking coffee, but now has the very different property of disliking coffee. A person can undergo qualitative change while retaining numerical identity. Since the self is supposed to be what explains numerical identity over time of persons, perhaps a self could undergo qualitative change. What it could not do is undergo numerical change—going out of existence and being replaced by another self.

If there is a self, it is "what makes me *me*," "the true me," that which "gives me my identity." These ways of describing what a self

---

1. The ambiguity of "same" is often resolved by context. When we say "*x* and *y* are the same P," what is meant is numerical identity. When we say "*x* and *y* are the same," what is meant is qualitative identity. So I might say that this is the same leaf as the one I showed you yesterday, meaning that they are one and the same leaf. Or I might say that this leaf is the same as the one that was on this branch last year, meaning that the two leaves are qualitatively identical. Other languages lack the ambiguity. In German, for instance, one says *das selbe* for numerical identity and *das gleiche* for qualitative identity.

is are all open to a common misinterpretation. People often speak of "discovering their self," of "finding their true identity." What they often mean by this is figuring out which of one's characteristics are most important or valuable to oneself. So someone might say that they have come to realize their identity isn't tied up with physical appearance but with less superficial things like artistic talent or communication skills. Discoveries like this are probably important to personal growth. But they have nothing to do with what the Buddhists mean by a self. We can see this from the fact that even if there is no self, we can still ask which of a person's characteristics are most important to that person's happiness. To speak of a self is to speak of some one part of the person, the part that must always exist as long as the person exists. To speak of an "identity" that can be "found" is to speak of characteristics or properties of what a person is like. There might very well be no single part of the person that must continue to exist in order for that person to continue to exist. (This is exactly what the Buddha is going to argue for.) But it might still be true that some characteristics of a person play a more important role in their life than others. Otherwise, it wouldn't make sense to say that a person has "lost their identity." Perhaps my life would be less meaningful if I were to lose those traits that now have the greatest importance to me. But it would still be my life. I could survive that qualitative change. I might be a very different kind of person. But I would still be me.

There is another misinterpretation that arises in connection with the idea that the self is what gives me my "identity." It is common to think that someone's identity is what sets that person apart from all others. Add to this the idea that one's identity consists in what one is like, one's characteristics or properties. The result is the notion that a self would be what makes one different from everyone else. Now the word "different" is ambiguous in the same way that "same" is: there is numerical difference or distinctness, and there is qualitative difference. If it's numerical distinctness that is meant, then it's true that the self would be what makes one different from others. If we have selves, then my self and yours must be two distinct things, not one. But it's not true if what's meant by "different" is qualitative difference. It is not true that if we had selves, each would have to be unique in the sense of being unlike every other. For all that is required of a self, two selves could be perfectly alike, like two peas in a pod, and still serve as what make one person numerically distinct from another.

The difficulty with the idea that the self must be qualitatively unique is that it once again confuses the notion of the self with the notion of what one is like, one's properties or characteristics. And properties may be shared between two things, whereas numerical identity may not. The leaf that is on this branch of this tree today might be exactly like the leaf that was here last year—same color, same shape, same pattern of veins, and so on. But they are numerically distinct leaves all the same. Perhaps no two persons are ever exactly qualitatively alike. Even twins who share the same DNA have physical differences, such as different fingerprint patterns. Still, there is no contradiction involved in supposing that there might be two persons who are exactly qualitatively alike. Imagine, for instance, that each of us has lived countless lives in the past. Given the innumerably many beings there would be in the universe, it does not seem unlikely that someone somewhere might once have lived a life just like the one I am now living. Yet that would have been someone else, not me. So if what makes me the person I am is my self, then my self is not what makes me qualitatively unlike other people.

Suppose, moreover, that each person is qualitatively unlike every other. This could be true even if there were no selves. Indeed it could be true if there were selves that were all qualitatively identical. This is actually the view of the self that many non-Buddhist Indian philosophers held. On their view, the self is something that is simple or impartite—it has no parts. The self is just the subject of experiences, the part of us that is aware of the different experiences we have. Your self and mine would then be just like those two peas in a pod. It's common to suppose that what makes different people qualitatively different is that they have different experiences. But on this view of the self, the different experiences that people have would not make their selves qualitatively different. Since the self is simple, while it is aware of its experiences, it cannot be changed by them. It is other parts of the person that are changed by those experiences. The experience of eating changes the shape of my body. The experience of smelling coffee strengthens a desire in my mind. On their view, my self is unaffected by these changes; it simply witnesses or is aware of them. Someone holding this view would say that the qualitative uniqueness of persons is explained by facts about those parts of the person that are not the self. Someone who denied the existence of a self could explain the qualitative uniqueness of persons in the same way.

There's a significant philosophical point in all this. It's important not to confuse the question of numerical distinctness with the question of how we tell two things apart. At least someone who held the philosophical position known as semantic realism would insist that these two questions not be confused. Semantic realists hold that whether a statement is true or false is determined just by the objective facts, independently of limitations in our understanding. So they would say that our inability to distinguish between two things tells us nothing about whether they are truly distinct things. The fact that two selves were qualitatively identical would mean we would be unable to distinguish between them. But this would not mean that they were really just one self. It could perfectly well be true that they are two numerically distinct things even though we could never tell them apart.

2.2 The Five *Skandhas*

In order to show that the self does not exist, we need to know what we are looking for and where to look. We now know that a self would be that part of the person that "I" is consistently used to refer to. So we can tell what to look for by seeing how we actually use words like "I." For instance, we say things like, "I was born in New York, but I lived in the Midwest for many years." So if "I" refers to the self, the self would have to be some one numerically identical thing that continues to exist throughout the past, present, and future history of the person. There are more clues to be found in the ways we use this word, but this tells us enough about what we're after for present purposes. Where should we look? Since the self is supposed to be a part of the person, we obviously need to look among the parts that make up persons. It would be helpful if we had a list of the basic categories of person-parts. This is just what the Buddha provides with his doctrine of the five *skandhas*. (The word *skandha* is here used in its sense of "bundle.") These are:

> *rūpa*: anything corporeal or physical;[2]
>
> feeling: sensations of pleasure, pain, and indifference;
>
> perception: those mental events whereby one grasps the sensible characteristics of a perceptible object, e.g., the seeing of a patch of blue color as blue;
>
> volition: the mental forces responsible for bodily and mental activity, e.g., hunger, attentiveness;
>
> consciousness: the awareness of physical and mental states.

A word of caution is necessary concerning these categories. Their names are here being used as technical terms, with precise definitions. Do not mistake them for the ordinary meanings of these words. For instance, the second *skandha*, feeling, refers only to the three kinds of hedonic sensation—pleasure, pain, and indifference (neither pleasure nor pain). It does not include most of the things that are often called "feelings," such as emotions like anger and jealousy. Those emotions

---

2. The literal meaning of *rūpa* is "form" or "shape," and you will sometimes see the word rendered as "form" in translations of Buddhist texts. But as the name of the first *skandha*, *rūpa* actually means "that which has form or shape," that is, anything material or physical. This is one case where it's best to stick with the Sanskrit original rather than try to come up with an acceptable English translation.

go under the very different *skandha* of volition. Likewise by "conscious-ness" is here meant just the awareness itself and not what it is that one is aware of. So when I am conscious of a pain sensation, there are two *skandha*s involved: the pain, which goes under feeling *skandha*, and the consciousness that is aware of it, which goes under consciousness *skandha*. Again, we sometimes use the word "perception" to refer to our beliefs about and attitude toward something. So someone might say, "My perception of the new government is that it is weak and will soon fall." This is not the sort of thing that would go under perception *skandha*: it is a complex set of mental states, whereas the things included in perception *skandha* are simple mental events. A perception in this technical sense is just the identification of a sensory content: the simple thought of a patch of blue or the smell of lemon.

The five *skandha*s are sometimes referred to collectively as *nāma-rūpa* (sometimes translated as "name and form"). Here *nāma* refers to the four *skandha*s other than *rūpa*. The literal meaning of *nāma* is "name," but here, it means "that which can only be named." The idea is that while *rūpa* can be perceived by the external senses, the mem-bers of the four other categories cannot be seen or touched. Because they are not publicly observable, we cannot explain what they are by pointing; we can only communicate about them through the names we have learned to use for these private states. What this tells us is that the doctrine of the five *skandha*s expresses a kind of mind-body dualism. The Buddha is claiming that in addition to those parts of the person that we can see and touch—the parts of the body—there are other constituents that are not themselves physical. Some philosophers today hold the view called physicalism, according to which all that exists is physical. On this view, there is no more to a person than the physical constituents, the body and brain. What we think of as mental events, such as thoughts and emotions, are really just complex brain events. When the Buddha says that in addition to *rūpa skandha* there are the four *nāma skandha*s, he is in effect denying that physicalism is true. On his account, mental events are separate non-physical kinds of things. We will be looking at this claim more carefully later on.

As we are about to see, the Buddha uses the doctrine of the five *skandha*s as a tool in his search for a self. He will go through each in turn and try to determine if anything included in that category could count as a self. Of course, we know he will claim nothing like that is to be found in any of the five. But this raises a new question: Would this really show that there is no self? Isn't it possible that the self exists apart from the five *skandha*s? In order for the Buddha's strategy to work, he will have to show that the doctrine of the five *skandha*s gives an exhaustive analysis of the parts of the person. We will call this the exhaustiveness claim.

> Exhaustiveness claim: every constituent of persons is included in one or more of the five *skandha*s.

In the following passage, the later commentator Buddhaghosa argues in support of this claim.

> The basis for the figment of a self or of anything related to a self, is afforded only by these, namely *rūpa* and the rest. For it has been said as follows:
> When there is *rūpa*, O monks, then through attachment to *rūpa*, through engrossment in *rūpa*, the persuasion arises, "This is mine; this am I; this is my self."
> When there is feeling, . . . when there is perception, . . . when there are volitions, . . . when there is consciousness, O monks, then through attachment to consciousness, through engrossment in consciousness, the persuasion arises, "This is mine; this am I; this is my self."
> Accordingly he laid down only five *skandha*s, because it is only these that can afford a basis for the figment of a self or of anything related to a self.
> As to other groups which he lays down, such as the five of conduct and the rest, these are included, for they are comprised in volition *skandha*. Accordingly he laid down only five *skandhas*, because these include all other classifications. After this manner, therefore, is the conclusion reached that there are no less and no more. (VM XIV.218)

This at least makes clear that Buddhists recognize the need to support the claim that there is no more to the person than the five *skandhas*. But it is not clear how good an argument this is. The idea seems to be that these are the only things we are aware of when we are aware of persons and so come to believe that persons have selves. Is this true? And if it were true, would it show that the exhaustiveness claim is true? We will return to this question.

2.3 Arguing for Non-Self from Impermanence

Let us now look at how the Buddha formulates his arguments for non-self. In the following passage, the Buddha is addressing his five former companion *śramaṇas*, in the episode we discussed in Chapter 1, §2. It contains two distinct arguments, which we shall have to prise apart. The first is what we will call the argument from impermanence since it is based on the claim that all five *skandhas* are impermanent or transitory.

> Then The Blessed One addressed the band of five *śramaṇas*:
> "*Rūpa*, O monks, is not a self. For if now, O monks, this *rūpa* were a self, then this *rūpa* would not tend towards destruction, and it would be possible to say of *rūpa*, 'Let my *rūpa* be this way; let not my *rūpa* be that way!' But inasmuch, O monks, as *rūpa* is not a self, therefore does *rūpa* tend towards destruction, and it is not possible to say of *rūpa*, 'Let my *rūpa* be this way; let not my *rūpa* be that way!'
> "Feeling . . . perception . . . volitions . . . consciousness, is not a self. For if now, O monks, this consciousness were a self, then would not this consciousness tend towards destruction, and it would be possible to say of consciousness, 'Let my consciousness be this way; let not my consciousness be that way!' But inasmuch, O monks, as consciousness is not a self, therefore does consciousness tend towards destruction, and it is not possible to say of consciousness, 'Let my consciousness be this way; let not my consciousness be that way!'"

"What do you think, O monks? Is *rūpa* permanent, or transitory?"

"It is transitory, Reverend Sir."

"And that which is transitory—is it painful, or is it pleasant?"

"It is painful, Reverend Sir."

"And that which is transitory, painful, and liable to change—is it possible to say of it: 'This is mine; this am I; this is my self'?"

"Certainly not, Reverend Sir."

"Is feeling . . . perception . . . volition . . . consciousness, permanent, or transitory?"

"It is transitory, Reverend Sir."

"And that which is transitory—is it painful, or is it pleasant?"

"It is painful, Reverend Sir."

"And that which is transitory, painful, and liable to change—is it possible to say of it: 'This is mine; this am I; this is my self'?"

"Certainly not, Reverend Sir."

"Accordingly, O monks, as respects all *rūpa* whatsoever, past, future, or present, be it subjective or existing outside, gross or subtle, mean or exalted, far or near, the correct view in the light of the highest knowledge is as follows: 'This is not mine; this am I not; this is not my self.'

"As respects all feeling whatsoever . . . as respects all perception whatsoever . . . as respects all volitions whatsoever . . . as respects all consciousness whatsoever, past, future, or present, be it subjective or existing outside, gross or subtle, mean or exalted, far or near, the correct view in the light of the highest knowledge is as follows: 'This is not mine; this am I not; this is not my self.'

"Perceiving this, O monks, the learned and noble disciple conceives an aversion for *rūpa*, conceives an aversion for feeling, conceives an aversion for perception, conceives an aversion for volitions, conceives an aversion for consciousness. And in conceiving this aversion he becomes divested of passion, and by the absence of passion he becomes free, and when he is free he becomes aware that he is free; and he knows that rebirth is exhausted, that he has lived the holy life, that he has done what it behooved him to do, and that he is no more for this world."

Thus spoke The Blessed One, and the delighted band of five
śramaṇas applauded the speech of The Blessed One. Now while
this exposition was being delivered, the minds of the five *śramaṇas* became free from attachment and delivered from the
depravities. (S III.66–68)

Here the Buddha cites two different sorts of reasons why the *skandha*s are not the self: they are impermanent ("subject to destruction,"
"transitory"), and they are not under one's control ("painful," "it is not
possible to say of *x*, 'Let my *x* be this way . . .'"). To separate out the
argument from impermanence from the second argument, let's ignore
the claims about the five *skandha*s not being under one's control (we'll
discuss this in §4) and focus just on the claims about their being subject
to destruction and transitory. If we add the exhaustiveness claim as an
implicit premise,[3] the argument is then:

1. *Rūpa* is impermanent.

2. Sensation is impermanent.

3. Perception is impermanent.

4. Volition is impermanent.

5. Consciousness is impermanent.

6. If there were a self it would be permanent.

IP [There is no more to the person than the five *skandha*s.]

C Therefore there is no self.

This argument is valid or logically good. That is, if the premises
are all true, then the conclusion will also be true. So our job now will
be to determine if the premises really are all true. But before we can do

_____

3. An implicit premise is an unstated premise that must be supplied for an
argument to work, and that the author of the argument did not state because
they thought it would be redundant—typically because it seemed to the
author to be common knowledge that the author and the audience shared.
We will follow the practice of putting implicit premises in square brackets.

that, there is one major point that needs clarifying: Just what do "permanent" and "impermanent" mean here? Once again, the doctrine of karma and rebirth becomes relevant. For those like the Buddha and his audience who accepted the doctrine, "permanent" would mean eternal, and "impermanent" would mean anything less than eternal. This is because if we believe it is the self that undergoes rebirth, and we also believe that liberation from rebirth is possible, then we will hold as well that the self is something that continues to exist over many lives and can even exist independently of any form of corporeal life. This may be what the Buddha had in mind with premise (6). And in that case, all that would be needed to show that x is not a self is to show that x does not last forever—even if it does last a long time. So if, for instance, the *rūpa* that is my body does not last forever, then it is not my self. And of course, my body does go out of existence when I die, so this would be sufficient to show that it is not my self.

What about those of us who do not accept the doctrine of karma and rebirth? To believe in rebirth is to believe that the person exists both before and after this life. If we do not believe in rebirth, then we may believe that the person exists only for a single lifetime. In that case, a self would not have to exist any longer than a lifetime in order to serve as the basis of a person's identity over time. So all that "permanent" in premise (6) could mean is "existing at least a whole lifetime." It could not mean "eternal." Likewise, to show that a *skandha* is impermanent in the relevant sense, we would have to show that it does not exist for the entire duration of a person's life. Does this mean that the argument won't work without the assumption of karma and rebirth? After all, isn't it true that our bodies last for our entire lives?

Not necessarily. First, we need to remember that the self is supposed to be the essential part of the person, and the body is a whole made of parts. Which of these parts—the organs that make up the body—is the essential one? There doesn't seem to be any single organ that I could not live without. Granted, I could not survive without a heart. But as heart replacement surgery shows, I don't need this heart in order to continue to exist. If my heart were my self, then when I got a replacement heart I would cease to exist and someone else would then be living in my body. That replacement heart came from someone else, so it would be that person's self. But surely, if I chose to have heart replacement surgery, I would not be committing suicide! What about the brain? Not only can I not live without a brain, there is no such thing as brain replacement surgery, so I cannot live without this brain. But here the problem seems to be entirely practical, not an "in-principle" difficulty. If we knew how to re-program an entire brain, then we might be able to replace a diseased brain with a healthy one while preserving all of a person's psychology. This would be like copying the contents of the failing hard drive of your computer, replacing the hard drive, then re-installing everything onto the new hard drive.

This brain-replacement scenario might seem too science-fictional to support premise (1). But there's a second reason someone might give for denying that the body is permanent in the relevant way. This is that all the parts of the body are constantly being replaced—at the level of the molecules that make up our cells. We're told that none of the atoms that made up our body seven years ago is among those making up our body now. Life processes such as metabolism and meiosis involve the constant, piecemeal replacement of the parts that make up a life-form. After this process has gone on long enough, all the matter making up a given organ is new: the atoms now making up my brain are numerically distinct from the atoms that made it up earlier. Given this, it could be said that the body and brain I have now are not numerically identical with the body and brain I had seven years ago.[4] *Rūpa* would then be impermanent in the relevant sense.

---

4. You might think that it would still be the same brain and body provided the molecules making it up were replaced gradually enough. But here is the sort of question a philosopher would raise at this point: Just how gradual is "gradual enough"? If swapping out all the molecules at once is not gradual enough, what about half? A third? Do you see how there might be a problem here?

We have been discussing how to interpret premise (6), the premise that a self would have to be permanent, and how premise (1), which says that *rūpa* is impermanent, might be true in light of our interpretation of (6). Our general practice in examining arguments will be to first look at what reason there might be to think that the premises are true and then to evaluate the argument overall. How might someone defend the remaining premises, (2)–(5)? These are not affected by the question of karma and rebirth in the way that premise (1) is. For regardless of whether we interpret "permanent" to mean eternal or just to mean lasting a single lifetime, the four *nāma skandhas* will all count as impermanent. This is the point the Buddha makes in the following passage:

> It would be better, O monks, if the uninstructed worldling regarded the body which is composed of the four elements as a self, rather than the mind. And why do I say so? Because it is evident, O monks, that this body which is composed of the four elements lasts one year, lasts two years, lasts three years, . . . lasts a hundred years, and even more. But that, O monks, which is called mind, intellect, consciousness, keeps up an incessant round by day and by night of perishing as one thing and springing up as another.
>
> Here the learned and noble disciple, O monks, attentively considers dependent origination: "This exists when that exists, this originates from the origination of that; this does not exist when that does not exist, this ceases from the cessation of that." O monks, a pleasant feeling originates in dependence on contact with pleasant objects; but when that contact with pleasant objects ceases, the feeling sprung from that contact, the pleasant feeling that originated in dependence on contact with pleasant objects ceases and comes to an end. O monks, an unpleasant feeling . . . an indifferent feeling originates in dependence on contact with indifferent objects; but when that contact with indifferent objects ceases, the feeling sprung from that contact, the indifferent feeling that originated in dependence on contact with indifferent objects ceases and comes to an end.

> Just as, O monks, heat comes into existence and flame into
> being from the friction and concussion of two sticks of wood,
> but on the separation and parting of these two sticks of wood
> the heat sprung from those two sticks of wood ceases and
> comes to an end; in exactly the same way, O monks, a pleas-
> ant feeling originates in dependence on contact with pleasant
> objects; but when that contact with pleasant objects ceases, the
> feeling sprung from that contact, the pleasant feeling that orig-
> inated in dependence on contact with pleasant objects, ceases
> and comes to an end. An unpleasant feeling . . . an indifferent
> feeling originates in dependence on contact with indifferent
> objects; but when that contact with indifferent objects ceases,
> the feeling sprung from that contact, the indifferent feeling that
> originated in dependence on contact with indifferent objects
> ceases and comes to an end. (S II.96f)

Of course, the Buddha knows that reflective people are more likely
to consider the mind than the body to be the self. In the Western
philosophical tradition, this is just what René Descartes did. He concluded that the true "I" is not the body but the mind—a substance
that thinks (i.e., is conscious), endures at least a lifetime and is imma-
terial in nature. Many Indian philosophers reached somewhat similar
conclusions. The Buddha's point is that the conclusion that the mind
endures at least a lifetime rests on an illusion. For what we call the
mind is really a continual series of distinct events, each lasting just a
moment, but each immediately followed by others. There is no such
thing as the mind that has these different events; there are just the
events themselves. But because they succeed one another in unbroken
succession, the illusion is created of an enduring thing in which they
are all taking place.

The eighteenth-century British philosopher David Hume said
something similar in response to Descartes. Descartes claimed to be
aware of the mind as something that is aware, that cognizes, perceives,
wills, believes, doubts—that is the subject of all one's mental activities.
Hume responded that when he looked within, all he ever found were

particular mental events, each of them fleeting, and never an enduring substance that has them. He concluded that it is just the relations
among those mental events that make us invent the fiction of the self
as an enduring subject of experience. The Buddha claims something
similar. And like Hume, he uses the relation of causation to support
his claim.

In the last chapter, we saw how the doctrine of dependent origination is used to explain the origin of suffering. In the passage we are
looking at, that doctrine gets put to a different use. The relation of
dependent origination is the relation between an effect and its cause
and conditions. Where this relation holds, the effect will arise when
the cause and conditions obtain, and the effect will not occur when
the cause and conditions do not. The Buddha asserts that all the *nāma
skandha*s originate dependently. He uses the example of feeling, but this
example generalizes to the other kinds of mental events as well. Consider the case of the feeling of pleasure I derive from eating my favorite
kind of ice cream. This feeling originates in dependence on contact
between my sense of taste (located in the taste buds on my tongue) and
the ice cream. Before there was the contact, there was no feeling of
pleasure, and when the contact ceases, so does the feeling. I may have
a feeling of pleasure in the next moment, but that occurs in dependence on a new event of sense-object contact—say, when I take my
next bite of ice cream. So that feeling is numerically distinct from the
first, for it has a different cause. One feeling has gone out of existence
and been replaced by another. Now the senses are by nature restless,
always making contact with new objects. This means that there will
be an unbroken stream of feelings and other mental events. It is easy to
mistake this stream for a single enduring thing. But the Buddha claims
that if we attend to the individual events making up this stream, then
seeing how they are dependently originated will help us overcome the
illusion of a persisting subject of experience.

The appeal to dependent origination is meant to show two things:
that there is no such thing as the mind over and above the mental

events making up the stream of consciousness; and that each of those events is itself very short-lived. Suppose we agreed with the Buddha on the first point. How successful is this appeal with regard to the second point? It is relatively easy to agree that feelings of pleasure and pain are transitory. We don't really need to use dependent origination to prove this. And since they are transitory, they could not be the self. Likewise for perceptions. But what about volitions? Granted, my desire for some new snack may last only as long as the effects of the ad I just saw. But we do seem to have volitions that endure, such as my desire for coffee. To this it could be replied that this is an acquired volition, one that I did not always have and might very well get rid of. So the opponent must look for volitions that seem to endure a whole lifetime. They might suggest what are sometimes called instinctual desires, such as the desire to escape life-threatening situations. Might this not be a volition that is permanent in the relevant sense? The Buddha will reply that what we are then describing is not one enduring volition but rather a pattern of recurring volitions, each lasting only a brief while before ceasing. This is shown by the fact that I only feel a desire to escape danger when I perceive a threatening situation. The desire thus originates in dependence on a specific sense-object contact event and ceases to exist when that event ceases. The opponent will then want to know what explains the pattern of recurring volitions. The opponent suspects that this pattern can only be explained by supposing that there is one enduring volition, a permanent desire to escape life-threatening situations, that is always present in me. My perception of a life-threatening situation brings the volition out into the part of my mind that is illuminated by consciousness, but it persists even when I am not aware of it.

Since we have no evidence that the Buddha was ever presented with this line of objection, we don't know how he would have responded. But later Buddhist philosophers do show us how it might be answered. What we have here is a certain phenomenon—a pattern of recurring desires over the course of a person's lifetime—and two competing theories as to how to explain the phenomenon. Call the opponent's theory the "in-the-closet" theory since it claims that some desires continue to exist hidden away in a dark corner of the mind when not observed. It explains the phenomenon by claiming that it is a single continuously existing volition that manifests itself at different times as the desire to duck a falling safe, the desire to dodge a runaway fertilizer wagon, and so on. The Buddhist dependent origination theory, by contrast, claims that these are many numerically distinct desires. It explains the pattern by appealing to the ways in which the parts of a person's body are arranged. Consider the thermostat that controls the heat in a house. It is because of the way in which the parts of the thermostat are put together that whenever the temperature goes below a certain threshold, the thermostat signals the furnace to go on. It is not as if the signal for the furnace to go on waits in the thermostat's closet until the room gets too cold. By the same token, the Buddhist would say, it is because of the way that the human body is organized that a danger stimulus causes a danger-escaping volition.[5] Now, this seems like a plausible explanation. It makes sense to suppose that it is, for instance, because of the way in which certain neurons in the brain are arranged that we have this desire to escape whenever we sense danger. But the in-the-closet theory also seems plausible to many people, so which should we choose?

There is a principle that governs cases like this. It is known in the West as Ockham's razor, but Indian philosophers call it the Principle of Lightness. For it dictates that we choose the "lighter" of two competing theories. It may be stated as follows:

---

5. No Buddhist text actually says this. This represents an extrapolation from what one school of Abhidharma says about continuity of karmic seeds during meditational states in which there is no consciousness. Their approach to that problem is dictated by their overall aversion to talk of dispositions or powers as real things. Given this attitude, it seems likely that this is what they would say about recurring desires.

Principle of Lightness: given two competing theories, each of which is equally good at explaining and predicting the relevant phenomena, choose the lighter theory, i.e., the theory that posits the least number of unobservable entities.

To posit an unobservable entity is to say that something exists even though we never directly observe that thing. Now you might think that positing an unobservable entity is always a bad idea. Why believe something exists when no one can see it or feel it? But modern physics tells us that there are subatomic particles like electrons and protons, and no one has ever seen or felt such things. Does that make modern physics an irrational theory? No. What the Principle of Lightness tells us is that we should only posit unobservable entities when we have to, when there is no better way to explain what we observe. We accept the theory that says there are subatomic particles because there is no other theory that does as good a job of explaining the phenomena. In the case of the phenomenon of recurring desires, though, things are different. We said that the in-the-closet theory and the Buddhist dependent origination theory give equally good explanations of this phenomenon. But the in-the-closet theory posits an unobservable entity that the dependent origination theory does not. The former theory says that volitions continue to exist in our minds even when we are not aware of them. The latter theory speaks instead of patterns of neurons in the brain—something that can be observed. This makes the latter theory lighter, and so it is the theory that we ought to choose.

The Principle of Lightness would help the Buddhist answer the objection about seemingly permanent volitions. It can also be used in defense of premise (5), the premise that says consciousness is impermanent. In the following passage, the Buddha claims that consciousness also originates in dependence on sense-object contact:

O monks, consciousness is named from that in dependence on which it comes into being. The consciousness which comes into being in respect of color-and-shape in dependence on the eye is called eye-consciousness. The consciousness which comes into being in respect of sounds in dependence on the ear is called ear-consciousness. . . . The consciousness which comes into being in respect of *dharmas* in dependence on *manas* is called *manas*-consciousness.

Just as, O monks, fire is named from that in dependence on which it burns. The fire which burns in dependence on logs of wood is called a log-fire. . . . The fire which burns in dependence on rubbish is called a rubbish-fire. In exactly the same way, O monks, consciousness is named from that in dependence on which it comes into being. The consciousness which comes into being in respect of color-and-shape in dependence on the eye is called eye-consciousness. The consciousness which comes into being in respect of sounds in dependence on the ear is called ear consciousness. . . . The consciousness which comes into being in respect of *dharmas* in dependence on *manas* is called *manas*-consciousness. (M I.259–60)

To this someone might object that we experience consciousness as some one thing that endures. That when I first see and then take a bite of ice cream, it is one and the same consciousness that is first aware of the color of the ice cream and is then aware of the taste of the ice cream. The Buddhist would respond by pointing out that there are periods in a person's life (such as during dreamless sleep) when there seems to be no consciousness at all occurring. If the opponent were to claim that consciousness continues to exist even then—only in the closet—the Buddhist could reply that their theory of dependent origination gives a lighter explanation of the apparent continuity of consciousness.[6]

But the Principle of Lightness would also help the Buddhist defend their claim that the mind is an invented fiction. As both the Buddha and Hume point out, we are never actually aware of the mind as

---

6. The Buddha's argument in the passage we just looked at is slightly different. It depends on the claim that there are six distinct kinds of consciousness, corresponding to the six senses and their respective objects. These twelve items (vision and the visible, hearing and the audible, etc.) are collectively referred to as the *āyatana*s.

something standing behind such mental events as feeling, perceiving, and willing. We are just aware of the feelings, perceptions, and volitions themselves. So the mind is unobservable. And it is the causal relations among these mental events that the Buddha says explain all the facts about our mental lives. So the mind becomes an unnecessary, unobservable posit.[7]

Why, though, should we accept the Principle of Lightness? The spirit behind this principle is the same as the spirit lying behind what we called semantic realism. Semantic realism says that the truth of a statement is not determined by such subjective factors as our interests or limitations in our cognitive capacities, but rather just by the objective facts. The underlying idea is that when it comes to finding out what the facts are, we should let the world outside our mind dictate what it is that we believe. To think that factors in my mind could determine what the facts are would, for the semantic realist, be to indulge in magical thinking. By the same token, they would say that positing unobservable entities is inherently suspect. Why believe that something exists when no one could possibly observe it? Because saying so makes it easier for us to explain what we do observe? This is letting what seems to us like a good explanation determine what we say the mind-independent facts are. This is letting our cognitive limitations determine what statements we believe are true. Magical thinking. The Principle of Lightness says we should resort to positing unobservable entities only when the world tells us we have no alternative.

We are now done with our review of the explicit premises in the argument from impermanence. There still remains the one implicit

---

7. Remember, though, that Early Buddhism is dualist. One can deny the existence of the mind and still be a dualist. The most familiar form of dualism is substance dualism, the view that there are two kinds of substance, physical substance and mental substance. Descartes was a dualist of this kind. Buddhists deny the existence of the mind. But they affirm the existence of mental events, such as feeling and perception, as things that are distinct from the physical (*rūpa*). While Early Buddhism denies substance dualism, it affirms what could be called event dualism.

premise, the exhaustiveness claim. If we accept this, then it seems we must say the argument from impermanence succeeds in establishing that there is no self. There is one important objection to the exhaustiveness claim. Many find this claim unacceptable because it leaves unexplained the sense we have that there is an "I" that has a body and various mental states. If the exhaustiveness claim were true, then while there would be a body and various mental states such as feelings and desires, these would not be the body and mental states of anyone or anything. They would be ownerless, states without a subject. And this strikes many as absurd. Is this a valid objection to the exhaustiveness claim, and so to the argument from impermanence? We will defer addressing this question. We turn instead to the second argument contained in the passage we have been investigating, the argument from control. This argument also relies on the exhaustiveness claim. Examining this argument will help us better frame the important objection to the exhaustiveness claim. We will then be better able to determine whether we should accept this claim and with it, the arguments that turn on it.

2.4 The Controller Argument

The argument from impermanence starts from certain ways in which we use the word "I." The argument from control has a different set of usages of this word as its starting point. We often say things like, "I feel OK about my hair today, but my nails look pretty ratty; I need to do something about them." This tells us that we think of the "I" as something that evaluates the state of the person and seeks to change those it finds unsatisfactory. Let us call this the executive function. Then if there is a self, the self would be that part of the person that performs the executive function. Recall that in the passage we looked at earlier, the Buddha says of each *skandha* that it cannot be the self because it is sometimes other than the way we want it to be. This makes it sound as if he is assuming that we would have complete control over the self, so it would always be perfect in our own eyes. And why would this be? If the self performs the executive function, then it tries to control the other parts of the person. But why must it have complete control over anything? And isn't there something odd about supposing that it exercises control over itself? Isn't the point of the executive function to exert control over other things? So far, the argument does not look very promising.

But this suggests that we need to look at the argument differently. Consider the following principle:

Irreflexivity Principle: an entity cannot operate on itself.

This principle is widely accepted among Indian philosophers. As supporting evidence, they point to the blade that can cut other things but not itself, the fingertip that can touch other things but not itself, and so on. Are there counter-examples to this principle, cases that show it not to be universally valid? What about a doctor who treats herself? The difficulty with this case is that when the doctor removes her ingrown toenail, it is not the ingrown toenail that does the treating, it is other parts of the doctor. Those who support the principle claim that all seeming counter-examples will turn out to involve one part of a complex system operating on another part. So there are no counter-examples, and the principle is valid.

Suppose this is right. Then if the self performed the executive function, it could perform that function on other parts of the person, but not on itself. This means I could never find myself dissatisfied with and wanting to change my self. And this, in turn, means that any part of the person that I can find myself disliking and seeking to change could not be my self.[8] Suppose, for instance, that I thought my nose

8. This way of interpreting the argument is suggested by the fact that the Sāṃkhya school of orthodox Indian philosophy gives an argument for the existence of the self that uses the same basic idea (though put to very different ends). See the comments on verse XVII in *The Tattva-kaumudi: Vācaspati Miśra's Commentary on the Sāṃkhya-kārikā*, Ganganatha Jha, trans. (Poona: Oriental Book Agency, 1957).

might be my self. My nose would then be the part of me that performs the executive function. When I evaluate the different parts of my body and mind, it would be my nose that did this. When I decided I didn't like something about my hair, or I tried to rid myself of some habit I disliked, this would be the nose's doing. The one thing the nose could never do is dislike and try to change itself. So if I ever found myself wanting to change something about my nose, that would show that my nose is not my self. And of course, I do dislike it when my nose itches, and I try to make it stop by scratching it. Therefore my nose is not my self. The argument as a whole will then go like this:

1. I sometimes dislike and seek to change *rūpa*.

2. I sometimes dislike and seek to change feeling.

3. I sometimes dislike and seek to change perception.

4. I sometimes dislike and seek to change volition.

5. I sometimes dislike and seek to change consciousness.

6. If the self existed it would be the part of the person that performs the executive function.

IP [There is no more to the person than the five *skandha*s.]

C Therefore there is no self.

Does this argument work? The first five premises seem to be true. There doesn't seem to be any observable part of the person that I could not find myself dissatisfied with and wanting to change. (Whether I succeed in changing it is another matter, but that's not relevant here.) We've seen how the irreflexivity principle comes in: if the self is the one part of me that's at work when I evaluate my states and try to change those I find unsatisfactory, then it is the one thing I could never evaluate and seek to change. So it looks like the argument does prove its conclusion provided the one implicit premise is true—that there is no more to me than the five *skandha*s.

At this point, it may strike you that there is something very peculiar going on here. On the one hand, we have an argument designed to

show that there is no part of the person that is the controller—no part
that performs the executive function. Yet in this very argument we
have premises stating, "I sometimes dislike and seek to change ___."
To say that I dislike and seek to change something is to say that I
perform the executive function. Yet, according to the conclusion of
the argument, there is nothing that performs the executive function.
If there really were no one in charge, then wouldn't the evidence that
is being used to show that no one is in charge really be bogus? Doesn't
the evidence presented in the premises actually require that the conclusion be false?

This suspicion can be developed into a very powerful challenge to the exhaustiveness claim. Here is how it goes. Suppose that
the five *skandhas* contain all the parts of the person that we ever
observe. We agree that we sometimes dislike and seek to change each of
the *skandhas*. And we also agree that whatever is performing this executive function cannot perform it on itself. The conclusion then seems
inescapable that there must be more to the person than just the observable parts, the five *skandhas*. And this "something else" must be the
self, the part that performs the executive function. This would explain
how it is possible to exercise control over all the observable parts of
the person without violating the irreflexivity principle. The controller
is itself unobservable. This could also be why Hume and the Buddha
were unable to find a self when they "looked within." The self is the
observer, and by the irreflexivity principle, it cannot observe itself;
it can only observe the other parts of the person, the five *skandhas*.
The exhaustiveness claim is false: there is more to the person than the
five *skandhas*. Not only do the Buddha's two arguments not succeed in
proving there is no self. The evidence they present actually turns out
to support the view that there is a self.

This is by far the most serious objection we have encountered to
the Buddhist arguments for non-self. Can the Buddhists mount a successful response? They will begin by pointing out an error in the opponent's characterization of the situation. In spelling out their objection

to the controller argument, the opponent said that the argument's conclusion is that there is nothing that performs the executive function.
But this is not what the conclusion of the argument says. It says there
is no self that performs the executive function. This leaves it open that
there might be something else performing that function. Or rather,
that there might be several somethings performing that function.
What the Buddhist has in mind is that on one occasion, one part of
the person might perform the executive function, on another occasion,
another part might do so. This would make it possible for every part to
be subject to control without there being any part that always fills the
role of controller (and so is the self). On some occasions, a given part
might fall on the controller side, while on other occasions it might fall
on the side of the controlled. This would explain how it's possible for
us to seek to change any of the *skandha*s while there is nothing more to
us than just those *skandha*s.

Consider this analogy. In a monarchy, there is the monarch, and
there are his or her subjects. A monarch is not their own subject; a ruler
rules over others, not themselves. Now in the case of Great Britain, it
is true that every living British citizen has been the subject of a British
monarch. But it is also true that Queen Elizabeth II is a British citizen.
How is this possible? If she is a British citizen, that means she has been
the subject of a British monarch. But she is the British monarch, and
by the irreflexivity principle she is not her own subject. Does this mean
that there is some unobservable meta-monarch presiding over the UK?
Of course not. Queen Elizabeth was the subject of her father, King
George, when she was still Princess Elizabeth before her father's death.

This shows us how it is possible for the following propositions all
to be true:

1. There is no more to the person than the five *skandha*s (the
   exhaustiveness claim).

2. I can perform the executive function on each of the *skandha*s.

3. An entity cannot operate on itself (the irreflexivity
   principle).

They can all be true because it need not be the same part of the person that performs the executive function on every occasion. So on one occasion, my nose might form a coalition with other parts of me and perform the executive function on my hair. On another occasion, a coalition with different members might perform the same function on my nose. We will call this the "shifting coalitions" strategy; it will prove useful to the Buddhist in other contexts as well. In effect, the Buddhist is claiming the opponent has forgotten the second possible meaning of "I." The opponent saw this word in premises (1)–(5) of the argument from control and assumed it meant a self, some single thing that exists as long as the person does. They assumed that when we say I can dislike and seek to change all the *skandha*s, it must be one and the same thing that does this evaluating and initiating on all of them. But "I" might also refer to all the parts of the person taken together. It might refer not to a self but to the person.

The Buddhist is not yet out of the woods, though. For one thing, we already know that the Buddha says the person is not ultimately real. We don't yet know just what that means, but it certainly doesn't sound like good news for the shifting coalitions strategy as a way around the objection. What's more, if "I" refers to the person, then the person should be one thing, not many. "I" is the first-person *singular* pronoun; "we" is the first-person *plural* pronoun. Yet, the strategy requires that it be different things that perform the executive function at different times. How is it that these distinct things all get called by a single name for one thing?

The Buddhist has an answer to this question. It is that "I" is what they call a "convenient designator," a word that refers to something that is just a useful fiction. The person is that useful fiction. The person is a whole made of parts. And wholes are not themselves real things; only the parts are. I think that "I" must refer to one and the same thing every time I use it because I have forgotten that the person is a useful fiction. I have forgotten that "I" is just a useful way to talk about all the parts taken together.

This is the basic strategy the Buddhist will use to finally answer the challenge to the exhaustiveness claim. But we need to investigate that strategy in much greater detail. Before we begin that task, it would be good to summarize the state of play to this point. The Buddha gave two arguments for non-self, the argument from impermanence and the argument from control. Both arguments relied on the exhaustiveness claim, which says there is no more to the person than just the five *skandha*s. This claim was crucial to both arguments since they both proceed by showing that there is some property of a self that all the *skandha*s lack. Showing this would not show there is no self if there could be more to the person than just these *skandha*s. The opponent objects that the exhaustiveness claim cannot be true if it is true that we can exercise some degree of control over all five *skandha*s. Indeed the opponent takes this fact to show that there must be more to the person than the five *skandha*s. The first Buddhist response is to point out that if the *skandha*s took turns performing the executive function, then all five could be subject to control without violating the irreflexivity principle. To this, the opponent objects that in that case, there would be not one controller but many. The second Buddhist response will be that there is a single controller, the person, but the person is only conventionally real. We now turn to an examination of just what this might mean.

2.5 "Person" As Convenient Designator

The passage we are about to examine comes from a work called *The Questions of King Milinda* (*Milindapañha*). It takes the form of a dialogue between a king, Milinda, and a Buddhist monk named Nāgasena. Milinda is a historical figure. He lived in the second century BCE, was of Greek ancestry (his Greek name was Menandros), and was among the rulers of Bactria (in present-day Pakistan) in the wake of its conquest by Alexander the Great. Milinda doubtless did discuss Buddhist teachings with Buddhist monks, but we don't know if there was someone named Nāgasena among them. The work was composed early in the first century CE, and it is probably not the transcription of an actual conversation. More importantly, it is not an early Buddhist work; it does not record the teachings of the Buddha and his immediate disciples. It is still useful for our purposes, though. For it is recognized as authoritative by a number of different Abhidharma schools. So its views represent a consensus position among a wide variety of commentarial traditions on the teachings of the Buddha.

The passage we are going to look at represents the first meeting of Nāgasena and Milinda. Notice how the conventional practice of exchanging names leads right to a substantive philosophical dispute.

> Then King Milinda drew near to where the venerable Nāgasena was; and having drawn near, he greeted the venerable Nāgasena; and having passed the compliments of friendship and civility, he sat down respectfully at one side. And the venerable Nāgasena returned the greeting; by which, verily, he won the heart of King Milinda.
>
> And King Milinda spoke to the venerable Nāgasena as follows: "How is your reverence called? Sir, what is your name?"
>
> "Your majesty, I am called Nāgasena; my fellow-monks, your majesty, address me as Nāgasena: but whether parents give one the name Nāgasena, or Sūrasena, or Vīrasena, or Sīhasena, it is, nevertheless, your majesty, just a counter, an expression, a convenient designator, a mere name, this Nāgasena; for there is no person here to be found."

Notice that his point here is not that his parents could have given him any of those other names instead. While this is true, it's not philosophically significant. His point is rather that whatever name he was given is just a useful way of labeling something that is not actually a person.

> Then said King Milinda, "Listen to me, my lords, you five hundred Yonakas,[9] and you eighty thousand monks! Nāgasena here

---

9. "Yonaka" is the Pāli name for the Greeks (Ionians) who ruled in the Punjab at this time.

says thus: 'There is no person here to be found.' Is it possible, pray, for me to assent to what he says?"

And King Milinda spoke to the venerable Nāgasena as follows: "Nāgasena, if there is no person to be found, who is it then that furnishes you monks with the priestly requisites—robes, food, bedding, and medicine, the needs of the sick? who is it that makes use of the same? who is it that keeps the precepts? who is it that applies himself to meditation? who is it that realizes the Paths, the Fruits, and Nirvāna? who is it that destroys life? who is it that takes what is not given him? who is it that commits immorality? who is it that tells lies? who is it that drinks intoxicating liquor? who is it that commits the five crimes that constitute 'proximate karma'? In that case, there is no merit; there is no demerit; there is no one who does or has done meritorious or demeritorious deeds; neither good nor evil deeds can have any fruit or result. Nāgasena, neither is he a murderer who kills a monk, nor can you monks, Nāgasena, have any teacher, preceptor, or ordination."

If there are no persons, there can be no one who gives alms to monks, nor can there be monks who embark on the path to nirvāna. Likewise, there can be none who commit evil deeds. These and other absurdities are what Milinda thinks follow from Nāgasena's claim.

"When you say, 'My fellow-monks, your majesty, address me as Nāgasena,' what then is this Nāgasena? Pray, sir, is the hair of the head Nāgasena?"

"Indeed not, your majesty."

"Is the hair of the body Nāgasena?"

"Indeed not, your majesty."

"Are nails . . . teeth . . . skin . . . brain of the head Nāgasena?"

"Indeed not, your majesty."

"Is now, sir, *rūpa* Nāgasena?"

"Indeed not, your majesty."

"Is feeling Nāgasena?"

"Indeed not, your majesty."

"Is perception Nāgasena?"

"Indeed not, your majesty."

"Is volition Nāgasena?"

"Indeed not, your majesty."

"Is consciousness Nāgasena?"

"Indeed not, your majesty."

"Are, then, sir, *rūpa*, feeling, perception, the volitions, and consciousness unitedly Nāgasena?"

"Indeed not, your majesty."

"Is it, then, sir, something besides *rūpa*, feeling, perception, volition, and consciousness, which is Nāgasena?"

"Indeed not, your majesty."

"Sir, although I question you very closely, I fail to discover any Nāgasena. Verily, now, sir, 'Nāgasena' is a mere empty sound. What Nāgasena is there here? Sir you speak a falsehood, a lie: there is no Nāgasena."

Notice that Milinda goes through each of the different parts of the body first, before coming to *rūpa*, or the body as a whole; in each case, he asks if this is what "Nāgasena" is the name of. He next asks about the four *nāma skandhas*. Nāgasena says "no" in each case, though he doesn't say why. We can imagine that he has the same reasons as those the Buddha gave in his two arguments for non-self. The next possibility Milinda suggests is the five *skandhas* taken collectively. It is noteworthy that Nāgasena denies this as well. The last possibility is that it is something distinct from all five *skandhas*. Nāgasena's denial is tantamount to the exhaustiveness claim: there isn't anything else. Finally, note that Milinda takes this all to mean that "Nāgasena" is a mere empty sound, a meaningless bit of nonsense. This is not what Nāgasena said the name is. He called it a convenient designator. These two views about what the name is have very different consequences. If Milinda is right that "Nāgasena" is a mere empty sound, then all the absurd consequences Milinda mentioned will follow. As we'll see in a bit, though, they don't follow if Nāgasena is right and the name is a convenient designator.

Nāgasena now tries to get Milinda to see the difference between a name's being a mere empty sound and its being a convenient designator. He does this by turning Milinda's own reasoning back on him, using the example of the word "chariot." Following his own reasoning leads Milinda into absurdities. He will then realize that the way out of those absurdities involves distinguishing between a word's being a mere empty sound and its being a convenient designator. The absurdities don't follow if we think of the word as a convenient designator.

> Then the venerable Nāgasena spoke to King Milinda as follows: "Your majesty, you are a delicate prince, an exceedingly delicate prince; and if, your majesty, you walk in the middle of the day on hot sandy ground, and you tread on rough grit, gravel, and sand, your feet become sore, your body tired, the mind is oppressed, and the body-consciousness suffers. Pray, did you come on foot, or riding?"
>
> "Sir, I do not go on foot. I came in a chariot."
>
> "Your majesty, if you came in a chariot, tell me what the chariot is. Pray, your majesty, is the pole the chariot?"
>
> "Indeed not, sir."
>
> "Is the axle the chariot?"
>
> "Indeed not, sir."
>
> "Are the wheels the chariot?"
>
> . . . .
>
> "Is the goading-stick the chariot?"
>
> "Indeed not, sir."
>
> "Pray, your majesty, are pole, axle, wheels, chariot-body, banner-staff, yoke, reins, and goad unitedly the chariot?"
>
> "Indeed not, sir."
>
> "Is it, then, your majesty, something else besides pole, axle, wheels, chariot-body, banner-staff, yoke, reins, and goad which is the chariot?"
>
> "Indeed not, sir."
>
> "Your majesty, although I question you very closely, I fail to discover any chariot. Verily now, your majesty, the word 'chariot' is a mere empty sound. What chariot is there here? Your majesty, you speak a falsehood, a lie: there is no chariot. Your majesty, you are the chief king in all the continent of India; of whom are you afraid that you speak a lie? Listen to me,

my lords, you five hundred Yonakas, and you eighty thousand
monks! King Milinda here says thus: 'I came in a chariot'; and
being requested, 'Your majesty, if you came in a chariot, tell me
what the chariot is,' he fails to produce any chariot. Is it possible, pray, for me to assent to what he says?"

When Nāgasena accuses Milinda of telling a lie, he is just driving
home to Milinda the consequences of following Milinda's reasoning
about the name "Nāgasena" when that reasoning is applied to the case
of the word "chariot." Nāgasena is being a skillful teacher. He wants
Milinda himself to come up with the resolution of the difficulty. This
is just what happens next.

> When he had thus spoken, the five hundred Yonakas applauded
> the venerable Nāgasena and spoke to King Milinda as follows:
> "Now, your majesty, answer, if you can."
> Then King Milinda spoke to the venerable Nāgasena as fol-
> lows: "Nāgasena, I speak no lie: the word 'chariot' functions as
> just a counter, an expression, a convenient designator, a mere
> name for pole, axle, wheels, chariot-body, and banner-staff."
> "Thoroughly well, your majesty, do you understand a char-
> iot. In exactly the same way, your majesty, in respect of me,
> 'Nāgasena' functions as just a counter, an expression, conve-
> nient designator, mere name for the hair of my head, hair of
> my body . . . brain of the head, rūpa, feeling, perception, the
> volitions, and consciousness. But ultimately there is no person
> to be found. And the nun Vajirā, your majesty, said this before
> the Blessed One:
>
> > Just as there is the word 'chariot' for a set of parts,
> > So when there are skandhas it is the convention to say,
> > 'There is a living being.'" (MP 25–28)

Notice how Milinda agrees that "chariot" is not a mere empty sound
but a convenient designator, a useful way of referring to the parts when
they are put together in a certain way. So when Milinda said he came
in a chariot; what he said was true, he was referring to something

real—just not a chariot. But why is this? Why not simply say that "chariot" is the name of a chariot? The answer is that a chariot is actually not a real thing. The parts are real, but the whole that is made up of those parts is not. The whole isn't anything over and above the parts. This is the view known as "mereological nihilism."[10]

This was the view of Early Buddhism. This view was systematically developed and argued for in Abhidharma. We will look at the argument when we investigate one of the Abhidharma schools (in Chapter 4, §1). In Early Buddhism, we just have what looks like a kind of ontological bias against wholes:[11] wholes are not really real, only the parts are. There is a way of making sense of that bias, though. Consider a set of all the parts needed to make a chariot. Suppose those parts are arranged in what we would call the "assembled-chariot" way: rim attached to spokes, spokes connected to felly, felly connected to axle, axle to body, and so on. In this case, we have one word that we apply to the set, "chariot." Now suppose those parts are arranged in a somewhat different way, which we might call the "strewn-across-the-battlefield" way: rim partly submerged in the mud, one spoke beneath a tree root, another spoke lying on the ground three meters to the northeast of the first, and so on. In this case we do not have a single name for the set. The best we can do is "all the parts that used to make up the chariot." This difference is reflected in another difference. In the first case, we think of the parts as one thing; in the second case we think of the parts as many things. Why this difference in attitude? Is it just because in the first case the parts are all in immediate proximity to one another? But if the parts were all jumbled together in a heap, we still wouldn't think of them as one thing, we'd think what we

---

10. Mereology is that part of metaphysics concerned with the relation between the whole and the parts. So mereological nihilism is the view that strictly speaking, there are no wholes, only ultimate parts.

11. Ontology is that part of metaphysics concerned with determining the basic kinds of existing things. When philosophers speak of 'an ontology,' they mean a list of the basic categories of existents. So, for instance, the doctrine of the five *skandhas* represents an early Buddhist ontology.

had then was just a bunch of parts in a pile. No, the difference in our ontological attitude (thinking of them as one thing in the one case but as many things in the other) stems from the fact that we have a single word for the parts in the first case but not in the second. And why do we have this single word in the one case? Because we have an interest in the parts when they are arranged in that way. When the set of parts is arranged in the assembled-chariot way, they serve our need for a means of transportation "across the hot sandy ground."

At this point, you might be thinking, "Well, of course. We only have a single word for the parts when they are put together in a way that serves our interests. This is no doubt why Nāgasena calls the word 'chariot' a convenient designator. Because it's convenient for us to have a way to designate the parts when they're assembled in that way. That configuration is one we're likely to encounter frequently (if we live in a society that uses chariots). And it's one we're likely to want to be able to refer to. It's much easier to tell your servant to fetch a chariot than to ask that they bring a rim attached to some spokes attached to a felly attached to . . . By contrast, it's much less likely that we'll ever need to refer to the set of parts when it's arranged in the strewn-across-the-battlefield way. And there are only so many words we can learn to use before our brains begin to seize up. If we had to learn a different word for every possible arrangement of those parts, our minds would melt. So we only have a single word in the case that serves our convenience. This all makes perfectly good sense. But why is it supposed to show that the chariot isn't really real?"

The answer is that our ontological attitude should not be dictated by our interests. Common sense says that the chariot is a real thing. Suppose we simply followed common sense. We would then be thinking of the chariot as one thing, but the same parts arranged in some different way as many things, because it was more convenient for us to think that way. And we all know what can happen when we let our needs dictate what we take reality to be like. Managing your finances that way can lead to disaster. This is why, strictly speaking, the chariot is not a real thing. It is just what Abhidharma will call a "conceptual fiction": something not ultimately real that is nonetheless accepted as real by common sense because of our use of a convenient designator. Here are some other examples of conceptual fictions we find in the literature: a house, a lute, an army, a city, a tree, a forest, and a column of ants. The list could be extended indefinitely. Our commonsense ontology is full of things that we think are real but are also wholes made of parts. The early Buddhist view is that strictly speaking, none of these things is really real.

Notice, though, that the word "chariot" is not a "mere empty sound." Apparently for Nāgasena, there is a difference between that status and a word's being a convenient designator. To call a word a mere empty sound is to say it has no meaning. And in this context, that would mean that there is nothing that it refers to. So if chariots are not really real, why isn't the word "chariot" a mere empty sound? We already gave the answer, but it is worth repeating and elaborating on. "Chariot" does refer to something, but not to what it appears to refer to. Its reference is misleading, for it seems to be the name of a single thing, a chariot, and there really is no such thing. It is, though, a useful way of talking about a set of parts when they are arranged in a certain way. So when we use the word correctly, there is something in the world that we are talking about. This is different from the case of a word that refers to nothing whatsoever, such as "sky-flower" or "son of a barren woman." (The Sanskrit equivalents of these expressions are both single words.) Since a barren woman has no children, there is no such thing as the son of a barren woman. So there is nothing that the word is the name of. Using the word "chariot" might help us get what we want, but using "son of a barren woman" never will. The chariot might be a fiction, but it isn't an utter fiction, like the son of a barren woman. Instead it's a useful fiction.

Nāgasena also calls the word "chariot" a counter, that is, an enumerative term like "dozen" or "six-pack." An enumerative term is a single expression that we use to refer to a collection of distinct things.

When we use terms like these, we are usually quite clear that there are just the many individual things and not an additional one thing that is made up of them. A carton of a dozen eggs is just the individual eggs; a six-pack of beer is just the six cans. To call a word like "chariot" or a name like "Nāgasena" a counter is to call attention to the fact that the same can be said about those expressions. They are nothing more than convenient ways of referring to a collection of things arranged in a certain way. We should not be misled by the fact that "the chariot" and "Nāgasena" are singular expressions. Just as a six-pack is six things, not seven, so a person is just the five *skandha*s, not those five plus something extra.

2.6 Two Kinds of Truth

There is one last point to make about the passage we have been looking at. Toward the very end, Nāgasena says, "Ultimately there is no person to be found." We can now see that he means to call the person a mere conceptual fiction, something we believe to exist only because of our use of a convenient designator. We will have much more to say about that in the next section. But we might ask what the force of this "ultimately" is. The answer is that it stems from a distinction between two ways in which a statement may be said to be true: ultimately and conventionally. What Nāgasena is saying is that it is not ultimately true that there are persons. He would, however, say that it is conventionally true that there are persons. The distinction may be characterized as follows:

> A statement is conventionally true if and only if it uses convenient designators and reliably leads to successful practice.

> A statement is ultimately true if and only if it corresponds to the facts and neither asserts nor presupposes the existence of any conceptual fictions.

Suppose there is a vending machine in the lobby of the building, and consider the statement, "There's a vending machine in the lobby."

You might think that what the statement says corresponds to the facts. But even if there is a sense in which that is correct, still it asserts the existence of a conceptual fiction, the vending machine. Does that mean the statement is ultimately false? No. To call it ultimately false is to be committed to the ultimate truth of the statement that is its negation, "There is no vending machine in the lobby." And for that statement to be true, it would have to be true that there are or at least could be such things as vending machines. It presupposes the existence of a conceptual fiction. No statement that uses the concept of a soft drink machine could be ultimately true. Our statement is conventionally true, though. Any speaker of English who was informed about the building would understand it since it uses convenient designators like "vending machine" and "lobby." And its acceptance can often lead to satisfaction of our desires, such as my craving for artificial sweeteners.

So any statement that uses convenient designators can only be conventionally true. It cannot be ultimately true, or ultimately false either. From the ultimate perspective, such a statement is simply without meaning, and so not the sort of thing that could be either true or false. The Sanskrit word (*saṃvṛti*) that we are translating as "conventional" literally means "concealing." And Buddhist commentators explain their use of this term by saying that convenient designators conceal the nature of reality. Words like "chariot" are misleading because they seem to refer to a single thing when they actually refer to a plurality: they present many things in the disguise of a one. If we want a complete description of how things actually objectively are, we should avoid using them. Of course, that objectivity would come at a steep price. If we could never use convenient designators in describing the world, then when we wanted to ride over the hot sandy ground, we would have to list all the parts that make up the chariot and describe how each is connected to the others. That would take a long time. So inevitably, we lapse back into using conventional truth.

This is not necessarily a problem, though. After all, not just any statement using convenient designators will be conventionally true.

The definition said such statements must reliably lead to successful practice. The statement about the vending machine might, but no statement about there being a teletransportation machine in the lobby will. There is no such thing as a teletransportation machine. But isn't it also true that there really aren't any vending machines either? Why should the belief in those non-existent things lead to successful practice? The answer, of course, is that there are all the suitably arranged parts that make up what we call a vending machine. It's because of their interactions that my desire for a cold dose of artificially sweetened, carbonated, flavored water gets satisfied. And if we wanted to, we could probably spell this all out. Usually, we don't want to. We just use our shorthand description of the situation: "There's a vending machine in the lobby." It's worth remembering, though, that standing behind every conventionally true statement is some (much longer) ultimately true statement that explains why acceptance of the conventionally true statement leads to successful practice. This connection between conventional truth and ultimate truth plays an important role in what follows.

2.7 Persons As Conventionally Real

The distinction between conventional truth and ultimate truth was developed by commentators on the early Buddhist texts in order to solve an exegetical problem. The problem is that there seems to be a major inconsistency in the Buddha's teachings. On some occasions, he teaches that there is no self and that what we think of as a person is really just a causal series of impermanent, impersonal states. On other occasions, he says nothing of this and instead teaches a morality based on the doctrine of karma and rebirth. The inconsistency stems from the fact that the latter teaching involves the idea that it is one and the same person who performs a deed in this life and reaps the karmic fruit in the next life. So the Buddha seems to affirm in those teachings what he elsewhere denies when he teaches the unreality of the self. Of course, we could simply agree that the Buddha contradicted himself and leave it at that. But the commentators saw a way around attributing such a major error to the founder of their tradition: the first sort of teaching represents the full and final truth, whereas the second rep-resents what ordinary people need to know in order to progress toward being able to grasp the full and final truth.[12] Using this distinction, commentators came to talk of those sūtras whose meanings are "fully drawn out" (nītārtha) as opposed to those with meanings requiring explication (neyārtha). The former came to be considered statements of the ultimate truth; the latter were said to be couched in terms of conventional truth.

The original point of the distinction between the two truths was, then, to clarify the early Buddhist view of the person. It was not to help us see that chariots are not ultimately real. It may not be too hard to see that chariots don't belong in our final ontology,[13] and that we think they are fully real only because of the way we talk. It would be much more difficult to believe these things about persons. As the following passage from Milindapañha makes clear, much careful work is needed before we can see how these things might be true. Nāgasena and Milinda have now been discussing the Buddha's teachings for a while.

---

12. This is said to be a manifestation of the Buddha's pedagogical skill (upāya-kauśala), his ability to fashion his teaching to the capacities of his audience. Presumably, the second sort of teaching is given to an audience that has not yet fully grasped the consequences of rebirth. They thus engage in immoral conduct, which only binds them more firmly to the cycle of rebirth. By teaching them a karmically based morality, the Buddha hopes to make them less prone to conduct that reinforces their ignorance. Then they will be better able to appreciate the full and final truth about persons. It is an interesting question whether this practice represents deception on the Buddha's part.

13. A "final ontology" is an ontology that makes no concessions to our interests and limitations, and accurately reflects the objective nature of reality. In early Buddhist terms, it would be an ontology that contains no mere conceptual fictions.

"Nāgasena," said the king, "is the one who is born that very person, or is it someone else?"

"He is neither that person," said the elder, "nor is he someone else."

"Give an illustration."

"What do you say to this, your majesty? When you were a young, tender, weakly infant lying on your back, was that you, the person who is now king?"

"Indeed not, sir. The young, tender, weakly infant lying on its back was one person, and the grownup me is another person."

Milinda's question is whether it is one and the same person who is born and then goes on to become an adult. Two things are worth noting. First, Nāgasena's answer is decidedly odd. How can the adult me and the infant me be neither the same person nor distinct persons?[14] Doesn't one or the other of these two possibilities have to be the case? Second, Milinda's answer is not what we would expect from someone whose views are supposed to represent common sense. Common sense says that adult and infant are the same person. Milinda says they are distinct persons. Here it's useful to bear in mind that Milinda has now been talking to Nāgasena for some time. One thing Milinda has learned is that all the *skandha*s are impermanent and that there is no self. He has concluded that a Buddhist should thus say adult and infant are distinct persons. Nāgasena will now show him why this common misinterpretation of non-self is wrong.

---

14. It would not be odd if what Nāgasena said was that while adult and infant are not the same qualitatively, neither are they numerically different persons. In fact, most people would say that's true. That baby and I are one and the same (numerically identical) person; but the baby had qualities I now lack, such as cuteness, so we are qualitatively different. This interpretation of "neither the same nor different" is only possible, though, if we translate what Nāgasena says using the ambiguous English "same" and "different." The ambiguity is not present in the original. It is numerical identity and numerical distinctness that he is denying.

"If that is the case, your majesty, there can be no such thing as a mother, or a father, or a teacher, or an educated man, or a righteous man, or a wise man. Pray, your majesty, is the mother of the zygote one person, the mother of the embryo another person, the mother of the fetus another person, the mother of the newborn another person, the mother of the little child another person, and the mother of the grownup man another person? Is it one person who is a student, and another person who has finished his education? Is it one person who commits a crime, and another person whose hands and feet are cut off [in punishment]?"

"Indeed not, sir. But what, sir, would you reply to these questions?"

Said the elder, "It was I, your majesty, who was a young, tender, weakly infant lying on my back, and it is I who am now grown up. In dependence on this very body all these different elements are collected together."

"Give an illustration."

"It is as if, your majesty, someone were to light a lamp; would it shine all night?"

"Certainly, sir, it would shine all night."

"But now, your majesty, is the flame of the first watch the same flame as the flame of the middle watch?"

"Indeed not, sir."

"Is the flame of the middle watch the same flame as the flame of the last watch?"

"Indeed not, sir."

"But then, your majesty, was there one light in the first watch, another light in the middle watch, and a third light in the last watch?"

"Indeed not, sir. In dependence on that first flame there was one light that shone all night."

. . . .

"In exactly the same way, your majesty, is the series of psychophysical elements (*dharmas*) connected together: one element perishes, another arises, seamlessly united as though without before and after. Therefore neither as the same nor as a distinct person does this latest aggregation of consciousness connect up with earlier consciousness." (MP 41f)

The overall point of the passage is clear enough: the ultimate truth about what are conventionally called persons is just that there is a causal series of impermanent *skandha*s. But there are several puzzling features that require close attention. First, there is Nāgasena's examples of the mother, the student, and the criminal. What point is he trying to make with these? Well, remember that Milinda thought the infant and the adult must be distinct persons. He thought this because he realized that the *skandha*s making up the infant are numerically distinct from those making up the adult. So he reasoned that in the absence of a self existing over and above the *skandha*s, adult and infant have to be two different persons. He is thus implicitly accepting a principle we might name after him:

> Milinda's Principle: numerically distinct *skandha*s make for numerically distinct persons.

What Nāgasena is doing is showing that we must reject this principle by showing that absurd consequences would follow if we accepted it.[15] It would, for instance, follow that there is no such thing as a mother. A mother is a woman who conceives and then bears a child and typically raises it to adulthood. So for there to be mothers, there must be persons who continue to exist from the time they conceive until the time their offspring is grown. But the *skandha*s making up a person are constantly going out of existence and getting replaced. For instance, the *skandha*s that make up the woman with an embryo in her uterus (second week of pregnancy) are numerically distinct from the *skandha*s that make up the woman carrying a fetus of six months. So by Milinda's Principle, these are distinct persons, and neither one

---

15. This strategy is called *reductio ad absurdum* or reducing to absurdity. The idea is to show that some statement should be rejected by first assuming that it is true and then deducing absurd consequences from that assumption. Since these absurd consequences are presumably unacceptable to everyone, this is supposed to show that we should not accept the statement in question. Indian philosophers call this strategy *tarka* or *prasaṅga*.

is a mother. Likewise, the *skandha*s that make up the student taking exams and the *skandha*s making up the student receiving a diploma are numerically distinct. So by Milinda's Principle the person who gets the degree is not the same person as the one who took the exams for that degree. The one who receives the diploma didn't do the work for it. Similarly, the *skandha*s that make up the convicted robber now sitting in prison are numerically distinct from the *skandha*s that held up the convenience store last year. So the prisoner is not the person who committed the crime; they don't deserve to be punished.

Milinda is quick to agree that these are all absurd consequences. But it is important to stop and consider why. When we think of ourselves and others as persons, we are thinking of a person as something that endures at least a whole lifetime. We are, in other words, gathering together all the *skandha*s from birth until death under one convenient designator, "person." Why would this practice be useful? The examples of mother, student, and criminal show why. If the pregnant woman didn't follow our practice but followed Milinda's Principle instead, she would not identify with the woman who will later give birth. So she would see no reason to follow her doctor's prenatal healthcare advice. The student who didn't identify with the graduate would see no reason to study for an exam that will only benefit the degree-holder. The criminal who didn't identify with the person who robbed the convenience store would see no reason to refrain from robbing again after getting out of prison.

Our concept of a person has it that persons endure at least a lifetime. If we followed Milinda's Principle, we would have to replace that concept with the concept of something that lasted nowhere near as long—perhaps for a day, but maybe for just a minute. (It depends on how long individual *skandha*s last and how many have to get replaced before we say we have a new whole.) To think of ourselves in that way would not be to think of ourselves as persons as we understand that concept. Let's call the resulting view "Punctualism," and the new concept of what we are "P-persons." What the examples show is that it would be a disaster if we thought of ourselves as P-persons rather than as persons. Our convenient designator "person" is convenient because it helps us avert this disaster. Why is this, though, if there really are no such things as persons? To think of yourself as a person is to think of yourself as a whole that is made up of all the *skandha*s that occur over a lifetime. And wholes like chariots and persons are mere conceptual fictions, not ultimately real things. So why should it work better to think of ourselves in this way?

The answer to this question lies in the point made in the preceding section. Statements that are conventionally true are ones that work. And for every statement that is conventionally true, there is some much longer, ultimately true statement that explains why it works. Nāgasena is making this point when he tells Milinda that adult and infant are the same person, and then goes on to say that past and present *skandha*s are united through their bodily causal connections. He is speaking first of what is conventionally true and then of what ultimate truth stands behind that conventional truth. But there was something else Nāgasena said about adult and infant, so let's look at all three of his statements.

1. Adult and infant are neither the same person nor distinct persons.

2. Adult and infant are the same person.

3. There is a causal series running from the "infant" *skandha*s to the "adult" *skandha*s.

We noted earlier that (1) seems odd. We can now add that (1) and (2) seem to contradict each other. (1) says that adult and infant are not the same person, while (2) says that they are. But perhaps we can now see a way out of both difficulties. Suppose we were to say that (2) represents the conventional truth, while (1)—and (3) as well—are supposed to be ultimately true. What (1) is meant to remind us of is that at the level of ultimate truth, no statement about persons could be true; all such statements are simply meaningless. To ask whether these are the same person or distinct persons is to assume that there are such things as persons. Since this presupposition is false, the question has no answer. Questions of personal identity simply can't arise at the ultimate level.

At the conventional level, though, we can say that I was that infant, that we are the same person. The examples of mother, student, and criminal are meant to show why (2) is conventionally true—because it works. And why does it work? As (3) tells us, the ultimate truth is that when the infant *skandhas* went out of existence, they caused child *skandhas* to come into existence, and so on in an unbroken chain until we arrive at the present adult *skandhas*. There are thus many causal connections between the *skandhas* existing at one time in the series and those existing later in the series. This, in turn, means that what happens to the earlier *skandhas* can influence how things are for the later *skandhas* in that series. Good eating habits early on make for well-functioning *rūpa skandhas* later. Excessive beer consumption tonight makes for pain sensations tomorrow. The desire to study now can bring about diploma-receiving behavior for later *skandhas* in the series. And so on. So when present *skandhas* identify with past and future *skandhas* in the series—when they think of those other *skandhas* as "me"—they are more likely to behave in ways that make it better for the later *skandhas*. To think of oneself as a person is to have the habit of identifying with the past and future *skandhas* in the series. This is why it is useful that we think of ourselves as persons.

Finally, Nāgasena gives another example of a causal series. This is a case where an unbroken chain of closely resembling particulars leads to a conceptual fiction, the one light that shone all night. When we look more closely at what we ordinarily think of as one light that endures an entire night, we see that it is really a series of short-lived flames. Each flame only lasts a moment, for it is composed of incandescent gas molecules produced by the burning of the oil. But when those molecules dissipate, they cause new ones to take their place.

For the heat of the first flame causes more oil to burn, producing a new replacement flame. So while each flame only lasts a moment, it causes another to take its place immediately upon its ceasing. The result is what looks like a single thing that endures from dusk till dawn. And so it is conventionally true that there was one light that shone all night. The reality, though, is that there are just the many numerically distinct flames, not the one light that has them. The ultimate truth is that there is just the unbroken succession of flames, each causing the next.

When it comes to the causal series of psychophysical elements,[16] Nāgasena gives an interesting description of the ultimate truth. The conventional truth is that I am a person who has existed for some time. I experience this existence as involving there being a "me" who is aware of the different experiences that this "I" has. Right now I am aware of reading these words and thinking about these ideas. Earlier, this same "I" was aware of other experiences—eating dinner, listening to music, talking with friends. The objects that this conscious thing is aware of vary over time, but it's always the same "I" that is aware of them. There is one thing, the "I," holding together a plurality, the experiences. This is how things seem to us when we use the convenient designator "person." The ultimate truth, though, is that there is a causal series of psychophysical elements. Each exists for a while, then goes out of existence, but causes a replacement element to come into existence. In some cases, the replacement resembles what was there a moment ago, as with the flames. Consciousness elements are like this. At each moment, there is a new consciousness, but each is qualitatively identical with its predecessor. In other cases, what follows an element does not resemble it. A feeling of pleasure gives rise to a desire, and that desire may, in turn, lead to other kinds of

---

16. The *dharma*s. These are the particular entities that get classified under the headings of the five *skandha*s. We will have much more to say about what these are in Chapter 4, §1.

experiences. This is the reality behind the appearance of a person living a life. There is no enduring "I" who has the different experiences. But neither does this mean that each experience is had by a distinct person. There are just the psychophysical elements and their causal connections. This is the reality that makes it useful to think of the series as a person living a life.

We are now in a position to return to the dispute over the exhaustiveness claim and the Buddha's two arguments for non-self. You will remember that both arguments relied on there being no more to the person than the five *skandhas*. The opponent objected to the argument from control on the grounds that our ability to exercise some degree of control over all the *skandhas* shows that there must be more to us than the five *skandhas*. The response was that there could be control over all the *skandhas* if it were a shifting coalition of *skandhas* that performed the executive function. But the opponent challenged this response on the grounds that there would then be many distinct I's, not the one we have in mind when we say that I can dislike and seek to change all the *skandhas*. We can now see how the Buddhist will respond. They will say that ultimately there is neither one controller nor many, but conventionally it is one and the same person who exercises control over first one *skandha* and then another. This is so because the controller is a conceptual fiction. It is useful for a causal series of *skandhas* to think of itself as a person, as something that exercises some control over its constituents. Because it is useful, it is conventionally true. This is how we have learned to think of ourselves. But because this person, this controller, is a conceptual fiction, it is not ultimately true that there is one thing exercising control over different *skandhas* at different times. Nor is it ultimately true that it is different controllers exercising control over them. The ultimate truth is just that there are psychophysical elements in causal interaction. This is the reality that makes it useful for us to think of ourselves as persons who exercise control. Our sense of being something that exists over and above the *skandhas* is an illusion. But it is a useful one.

2.8 Non-Self and Rebirth

Does this strategy succeed in defending the exhaustiveness claim against the opponent's attack? I shall leave it as an exercise for the reader to answer this question. For there is a very different objection to the arguments for non-self that we need to examine. Perhaps you have been wondering how, given his belief in rebirth, the Buddha could have argued for the non-existence of a self. How is rebirth possible if there is no self that gets reborn, that goes from one life to the next?

Notice that this is a very different sort of objection than the one against the exhaustiveness claim. That objection tried to show that a key premise in the two arguments for non-self is false. This one doesn't do that. Instead, it tries to show that the conclusion of the arguments (that there is no self) is incompatible with something else that the Buddha believes (that there is rebirth). If these two things really are incompatible, then the Buddhist could respond in either of two ways: by accepting a self or by abandoning belief in rebirth. Given the centrality of non-self to the Buddha's teachings, the latter might seem the better choice. But the Buddhist will say that we don't need to choose. For there is no incompatibility between non-self and rebirth; rebirth is not transmigration. This is the point Nāgasena makes in the following:

> Said the king: "Nāgasena, does rebirth take place without anything transmigrating [passing over]?"
>
> "Yes, your majesty. Rebirth takes place without anything transmigrating."
>
> "How, Nāgasena, does rebirth take place without anything transmigrating? Give an illustration."
>
> "Suppose, your majesty, a man were to light a light from another light; pray, would the one light have passed over [transmigrated] to the other light?"
>
> "Indeed not, sir."
>
> "In exactly the same way, your majesty, does rebirth take place without anything transmigrating."
>
> "Give another illustration."

"Do you remember, your majesty, having learnt, when you were a boy, some verse or other from your poetry teacher?"

"Yes, sir."

"Pray, your majesty, did the verse pass over [transmigrate] to you from your teacher?"

"Indeed not, sir."

"In exactly the same way, your majesty, does rebirth take place without anything transmigrating."

"You are an able man, Nāgasena." (MP 71)

In both examples, we have a causal process whereby one thing brings about the arising of some distinct but similar thing: a lit candle serves as cause of there being a lit oil lamp, and the teacher's knowledge of the poem serves as cause of the student's knowing the poem. The idea, then, is that rebirth occurs when one set of *skandha*s, those making up the person in this life, causes a new set of *skandha*s to come into existence in the circumstances of a new life. This is not different in kind from the sort of thing that regularly occurs during a single lifetime. The cells in our bodies constantly wear out and die, but give rise to similar replacements. Desires, in getting satisfied and so being exhausted, set the stage for similar future desires. The continued existence of a person over the course of a lifetime is just the occurrence of a causal series of impermanent *skandha*s.

There are, of course, important differences between the case of a single lifetime and the case of rebirth. While qualitative changes occur during a life, they are gradual. I might wake up with a few more gray hairs than I had yesterday, but I never wake up to find I've become a cow. It is thought possible, though, to die as a human and be reborn as a cow. Unless I'm riding in a train or flying, I don't go to sleep in one place and wake up in another. Typically, though, one is said to be reborn somewhere other than where one died. I can usually remember what I did yesterday, but one doesn't typically remember the events from one's past lives. Still, the process of rebirth is governed by causal laws, namely the laws of karma. It is because I did these things out of these desires that I am reborn into this kind of life. In the case of a single lifetime, it is because the distinct psychophysical elements are causally connected that it is useful to collect them all together under the convenient designator "person." The same goes for the *skandha*s in distinct lives. It is true that we expect an effect to occur at the same place as the cause, and rebirth often occurs far from the place of death. But, it is pointed out, a magnet can cause changes at some distance.

There may be another worry at work here. Rebirth is supposed to be governed by karmic causal laws. And karma is supposed to represent a kind of natural justice: people get what they deserve, good rebirth for virtuous actions, bad rebirth for vicious actions. And how can it be just if it isn't one and the same thing that performs the action and then gets the reward or punishment? This is something that bothers Milinda:

> "Nāgasena," said the king, "what is it that is born into the next existence?"
>
> "Your majesty," said the elder, "it is *nāma* and *rūpa* that is born into the next existence."
>
> "Is it this same *nāma* and *rūpa* that is born into the next existence?"
>
> "Your majesty, it is not this same *nāma* and *rūpa* that is born into the next existence; but with this *nāma* and *rūpa*, your majesty, one does a deed—it may be good, or it may be evil—and by reason of this deed another *nāma* and *rūpa* is born into the next existence."
>
> "Sir, if it is not this same *nāma* and *rūpa* that is born into the next existence, is one not freed from one's deeds?"
>
> "If one were not born into another existence," said the elder, "one would be freed from one's evil deeds; but, your majesty, inasmuch as one is born into another existence, therefore is one not freed from one's evil deeds."
>
> "Give an illustration."
>
> "Your majesty, it is as if a man were to light a fire in the winter-time and warm himself, and were to go off without putting it out. And then the fire were to burn another man's field, and the owner of the field were to seize him, and show him to the

king, and say, 'Sir, this man has burnt up my field'; and the other
were to say, 'Sir, I did not set this man's field on fire. The fire
which I failed to put out was a different one from the one which
burnt up this man's field. I am not liable to punishment.' Pray,
your majesty, would the man be liable to punishment?"

"Assuredly, sir, he would be liable to punishment."

"For what reason?"

"Because, in spite of what he might say, the man would be
liable to punishment for the reason that the last fire derived
from the first fire."

"In exactly the same way, your majesty, with this *nāma* and
rūpa one does a deed—it may be good, or it may be wicked—and
by reason of this deed another *nāma* and *rūpa* is born into the
next existence. Therefore is one not freed from one's evil deed."

The point should be clear. In the case of the fire, strictly speaking the
wood fire that the man lit to warm himself is not the grass fire that
consumed the other man's field. A fire that depends on one kind of fuel
cannot be numerically identical with a fire that depends on another
kind of fuel. But since the one fire caused the other, it is conventionally true that the first man burnt the second man's field. Likewise,
the psychophysical elements involved in the performance of a vicious
deed are ultimately distinct from the psychophysical elements born
into the painful circumstances of a *preta*. Suppose I'm the one who did
the vicious deed. If I die without ever being punished, does the fact
that nothing transmigrates mean that I escape getting what I deserve?
No. Since these human *skandha*s caused those *preta skandha*s, it is conventionally true that that *preta* will be me, the one who did the deed. I
will get what I deserve.[17]

---

17. Notice that this case is not different in kind from the case of the convicted
criminal that Milinda asked about earlier. That was a case of human justice,
while this is a case of natural justice. And in that case, justice got carried out in a
single lifetime, while this requires two lives. But the principle is the same: where
there are the right kinds of causal connections, it is conventionally true that
punishment is deserved even when ultimately distinct *skandha*s are involved.

This is how the Buddhist defends the doctrine of karma and rebirth against the charge that it is incompatible with non-self. Of course, you might think that karma and rebirth are implausible beliefs that a reasonable Buddhist would abandon. The point here is just that the theory of two truths and the claim that persons are conventionally real may be used to show that rebirth and non-self are not incompatible. If Buddhists ought to stop believing in rebirth, it is not because that belief is inconsistent with their central tenet that there is no self.

There are still some questions that the Buddhist needs to answer. The most important of these is this. The early Buddhist defense of non-self makes crucial use of the claim that wholes are unreal. This was the basis for their claim that persons are mere conceptual fictions that are only conventionally real. When we discussed the case of the chariot, perhaps it occurred to you that a spoke is also a whole made of parts. A spoke consists of many particles of metal or wood. So if wholes are only conceptual fictions, the spoke can't be ultimately real either. The only things that could be ultimately real would have to be impartite things, partless parts. And just what are they like? Behind this question may lurk the suspicion that there is nothing that is genuinely impartite. That would represent a major difficulty for the Buddhist approach. The Abhidharma schools of Buddhist philosophy tried to solve this difficulty. In Chapter 4, we will look at an Abhidharma attempt to work out what the ultimately real impartite entities are like.

Before we do that, though, we will look at the ethical consequences of the doctrine of non-self. In the last chapter, we wondered what it might be like to achieve the Buddhist goal of enlightenment. We now know more about what it would be like. To be enlightened is to know that strictly speaking there is no "me" but only impersonal impermanent psychophysical elements in a causal series. It is to know that the "I" is just a conceptual fiction. What might it be like to live with that knowledge? Would it be liberating, or would it be depressing? And how might it affect my behavior toward others? Would it make me more concerned about their welfare? Or would I figure that since there are no persons, I needn't worry about infringing on their rights? Would I conclude that anything goes? These are some of the questions we will address in the next chapter.

Some Key Points of This Chapter

- To say there is no self is to say that persons lack an essence, some one part that is thought necessary to the continued existence of the person (the part that makes me *me*).

- Persons are said to be composed of five kinds of constituents, the five *skandha*s.

- The Buddha gave two arguments for non-existence of a self, the argument from impermanence and the controller argument.

- Both arguments depend on the assumption that there is no more to the person than the five *skandha*s (the exhaustiveness claim).

- One strategy for defending the exhaustiveness claim involves saying that words like "person" and "I" are mere convenient designators, useful ways of referring to what are actually just collections of *skandha*s.

- This strategy relies on mereological nihilism, the view that there are no wholes and what we think of as a whole (e.g., a chariot) is really no more than just the parts.

- Buddhists claim there are two ways a statement can be true, conventionally and ultimately: statements that use convenient designators like "chariot" or "person" can only be conventionally true, while statements using only words that refer to *skandha*s can be ultimately true.

- Since "person" is a convenient designator for a causal series of *skandha*s, it can be conventionally true that persons are reborn even though ultimately nothing transmigrates from one life to the next.

For Further Reading

The complete debate between Nāgasena and King Milinda may be found in T. W. Rhys Davids, trans., *The Questions of King Milinda*, (Oxford University Press, 1890; Delhi: Motilal Banarsidass, 1965).

For discussion of Ockham's razor and its use in scientific theory construction, see E. C. Barnes, "Ockham's Razor and the Anti-Superfluity Principle," *Erkenntnis* 53, no. 3 (2000): 353–74.

Chapter Three

Buddhist Ethics

The view of persons that we discussed in the last chapter is a form of reductionism. To be a reductionist about a certain kind of thing is to hold that things of that kind do not exist in the strict sense, that their existence just consists in the existence of other kinds of things. The Buddhist view of non-self, for instance, says that the existence of a person just consists in the occurrence of a complex causal series of impermanent, impersonal *skandha*s. But Buddhists are not the only ones to hold a reductionist view of persons. On some interpretations, two early modern British philosophers, John Locke and David Hume, held such a view. More recently, Derek Parfit has given a sophisticated defense of reductionism about persons, which he explains as the denial that the continued existence of a person involves any "further fact" over and above the facts about a causal series of psychophysical elements. Here is what he says about the effects of coming to believe that the reductionist view is true of oneself:

> Is the truth depressing? Some may find it so. But I find it liberating, and consoling. When I believed that my existence was such a further fact, I seemed imprisoned in myself. My life seemed like a glass tunnel, through which I was moving faster every year, and at the end of which there was darkness. When I changed my view, the walls of my glass tunnel disappeared. I now live in the open air. There is still a difference between my life and the lives of other people. But the difference is less. Other people are closer. I am less concerned about the rest of my life, and more concerned about the lives of other people. (1984: 281)

Buddhists say something similar. They say that becoming enlightened, coming to know the truth of reductionism, relieves existential suffering. They also claim that it makes us more concerned about the welfare of others. In this chapter, we will explore how that might be. Ethics is concerned with questions concerning how we ought to act: how we should live our own lives and how we should act toward others. Buddhists are reductionists about persons: they claim there is no self and that persons are only conventionally real. We will be investigating the ethical consequences of this claim.

3.1 Can Nirvāna Be Described?

We saw earlier (in §1 of the Introduction) that philosophical traditions often begin with a quest for answers to the question of how we should live our lives. For Early Buddhism, the answer is clearly that we should seek nirvāna, the cessation of suffering. We saw in Chapter 1 that this claim is based at least in part on the notion that only by becoming enlightened can we hope to permanently escape existential suffering. But it was unclear at that point whether there is anything more to being enlightened than just being without suffering. Is nirvāna pleasant? Is it a state of well-being or happiness? The early Buddhist texts are mostly silent on this point. We saw, though, that this might be part of a strategy to get around the paradox of liberation. But in that case, there should be more that can be said about what nirvāna is like. What we have since learned about the Buddhist doctrine of non-self—about what it is that Buddhists think we most fundamentally are—might help us better understand why Buddhists think nirvāna should be our ultimate aim.

You will sometimes encounter the claim that Buddhist nirvāna is ineffable, that it simply cannot be described or understood, it can only be experienced. If this were right, then there would be no point in our pursuing the question of what nirvāna is like. If we were trying to decide whether to seek it ourselves or not, we would be stuck. We would have to simply take the word of those who have attained it that it is supremely valuable. We would have to embark on the path without knowing for ourselves where it went. But this claim is based on a misunderstanding of what is said about the *arhat* (enlightened person) in early Buddhist texts like the following.

> Vaccha the *śramana* spoke to the Blessed One as follows: "How is it, Gotama? Does Gotama hold that the *arhat* exists after death, and that this view alone is true, and every other false?"
>
> "No, Vaccha. I do not hold that the *arhat* exists after death, and that this view alone is true, and every other false."
>
> "How is it, Gotama? Does Gotama hold that the *arhat* does not exist after death, and that this view alone is true, and every other false?"
>
> "No, Vaccha. I do not hold that the *arhat* does not exist after death, and that this view alone is true, and every other false."
>
> "How is it, Gotama? Does Gotama hold that the *arhat* both exists and does not exist after death, and that this view alone is true, and every other false?"
>
> "No, Vaccha. I do not hold that the *arhat* both exists and does not exist after death, and that this view alone is true, and every other false."
>
> "But how is it, Gotama? Does Gotama hold that the *arhat*, neither exists nor does not exist after death, and that this view alone is true, and every other false?"
>
> "No, Vaccha, I do not hold that the *arhat* neither exists nor does not exist after death, and that this view alone is true, and every other false."
>
> "Vaccha, the theory that the *arhat* exists after death is a jungle, a wilderness, a puppet-show, a writhing, and a fetter, and is coupled with misery, ruin, despair, and agony, and does not tend to aversion, absence of passion, cessation, quiescence, knowledge, supreme wisdom, and nirvāna. . . .
>
> "Vaccha, the theory that the *arhat* neither exists nor does not exist after death is a wilderness . . . and does not tend to . . . supreme wisdom, and nirvāna.
>
> "This is the objection I perceive to these theories, so that I have not adopted any one of them."
>
> "But has Gotama any theory of his own?"

"The Tathāgata, O Vaccha, is free from all theories; but this, Vaccha, the Tathāgata does know: the nature of *rūpa*, and how *rūpa* arises, and how *rūpa* perishes; the nature of sensation. . . . the nature of consciousness, and how consciousness arises, and how consciousness perishes. Therefore say I that the Tathāgata has attained deliverance and is free from attachment, inasmuch as all imaginings, or agitations, or false notions concerning a self or anything pertaining to a self have perished, have faded away, have ceased, have been given up and relinquished."

"But, Gotama, where is the monk reborn who has attained to this deliverance for his mind?"

"Vaccha, to say that he is reborn would not fit the case."

"Then, Gotama, he is not reborn."

"Vaccha, to say that he is not reborn would not fit the case."

"Then, Gotama, he is both reborn and is not reborn."

"Vaccha, to say that he is both reborn and not reborn would not fit the case."

"Then, Gotama, he is neither reborn nor not reborn."

"Vaccha, to say that he is neither reborn nor not reborn would not fit the case. . . ."

"Gotama, I am at a loss what to think in this matter, and I have become greatly confused, and the faith in Gotama inspired by an earlier conversation has now disappeared."

"Enough, O Vaccha! Be not at a loss what to think in this matter, and be not greatly confused. Profound, O Vaccha, is this doctrine, recondite, and difficult of comprehension, good, excellent, and not to be reached by mere reasoning, subtle, and intelligible only to the wise; and it is a hard doctrine for you to learn, who belong to another sect, to another faith, to another persuasion, to another discipline, and sit at the feet of another teacher. Therefore, Vaccha, I will now question you, and answer as you think right. What do you think, Vaccha? Suppose a fire were to burn in front of you; would you be aware that the fire was burning in front of you?"

"Gotama, if a fire were to burn in front of me, I should be aware that a fire was burning in front of me."

"But suppose, Vaccha, someone were to ask you, 'On what does this fire that is burning in front of you depend?' What would you answer, Vaccha?"

"Gotama, if someone were to ask me, 'On what does this fire that is burning in front of you depend?' I would answer, Gotama, 'It is on fuel of grass and wood that this fire that is burning in front of me depends.'"

"But, Vaccha, if the fire in front of you were to become extinct, would you be aware that the fire in front of you had become extinct?"

"Gotama, if the fire in front of me were to become extinct, I should be aware that the fire in front of me had become extinct."

"But, Vaccha, if someone were to ask you, 'In which direction has that fire gone: east, or west, or north, or south?' what would you say, O Vaccha?"

"The question would not fit the case, Gotama. For the fire which depended on fuel of grass and wood, when that fuel has all gone, and it can get no other, being thus without nutriment, is said to be extinct."

"In exactly the same way, Vaccha, all *rūpa* by which one could predicate the existence of the *arhat*, all that *rūpa* has been abandoned, uprooted, pulled out of the ground like a palmyra-tree, and become non-existent and not liable to spring up again in the future. The *arhat*, O Vaccha, who has been released from what is styled *rūpa*, is deep, immeasurable, unfathomable, like the mighty ocean. To say that he is reborn would not fit the case. To say that he is not reborn would not fit the case. To say that he is both reborn and not reborn would not fit the case. To say that he is neither reborn nor not reborn would not fit the case.

"All sensation . . .

"All perception . . .

"All volition. . . . All consciousness by which one could predicate the existence of the *arhat*, all that consciousness has been abandoned, uprooted, pulled out of the ground like a palmyra-tree, and become non-existent and not liable to spring up again in the future. . . . To say that he is not reborn would not fit the case. To say that he is both reborn and not reborn would not fit the case. To say that he is neither reborn nor not reborn would not fit the case." (M I.483–38)

It should be clear how passages like this might lead some to think that the state of nirvāna is ineffable. First, we find the Buddha denying that any of the four possibilities listed by Vaccha correctly describes the situation of the *arhat* after death. Then he says that this situation is "deep" and "immeasurable." Since logic suggests that one of the four possibilities would have to be true,[1] the conclusion seems inescapable that the Buddha is calling nirvāna something that transcends all rational discourse. But now that we understand the distinction between the two truths, we can see why this would be a mistake. For as the example of the fire makes clear, the Buddha's four denials all have to do with the fact that any statement about the enlightened person lacks meaning at the level of ultimate truth.

When a fire has exhausted its fuel, we say that it's gone. Where has it gone? The question makes no sense. For the extinguished fire to have gone somewhere, it would have to continue to exist. The question presupposes the continued existence of the fire. Yet, the question still seems to be meaningful. Since we are saying something about the fire—that it is extinguished—must there not be a real fire that we are talking about? How can you talk about something that is utterly unreal? And since this real fire is not here in front of us, must it not be somewhere else? When we encounter this sort of paradoxical situation, it is useful to stop and ask about the nature of the words we are using.

---

1. Actually, logic seems to suggest that there are only two possibilities, not four. There are a number of so-called disputed questions where the Buddha considers four possible answers: P, not P, both P and not P, and neither P nor not P. This general form or scheme is called the tetralemma (*catuṣkoṭi*). But logic seems to limit us to just a dilemma: either "P" is true, or else it is false, in which case "not P" is true. Scholars have disputed whether the presence of the third and fourth possibilities in this scheme indicates that Buddhists use some kind of alternative logic. One plausible answer is that the logic is standard. The third possibility (both P and not P) is meant to cover cases where "P" is ambiguous so that it could be said to be true in one sense but false in another. And the fourth possibility is meant to cover cases where there genuinely exists some third possibility besides those of "P" and "not P," such as the possibility that the situation is simply indescribable.

How does the word "fire" actually function? Consider the situation where we say we kept the fire burning by adding more fuel. Here we are talking as if there is one enduring thing, the fire, that first consists of flames from kindling, then later consists of flames from logs, then still later consists of flames from new logs. This should tell us that "fire" is a convenient designator for a causal series of flames (just as "the one light that shone all night" was really a causal series of lamp flames). And this, in turn, means that no statement using the word "fire" can be ultimately true (or ultimately false). Any such statement lacks meaning at the ultimate level of truth. All that can be talked about at the ultimate level are individual flames, not the series of flames as a whole. This is why no answer to the question of where the fire has gone is true. For a statement to be true (or false), it has to be meaningful. And statements about mere conceptual fictions are not ultimately meaningful.

When we apply this analysis to the case of the *arhat* after death, it becomes clear why the Buddha can reject all four possibilities without implying that nirvāna is an ineffable state. The word *arhat* is a convenient designator, just like "fire." So nothing we say about the *arhat* can be ultimately true. The only ultimately true statement about the situation will be one that describes the *skandha*s in the causal series. It is, for instance, true that at a certain point (which we conventionally call "the death of the *arhat*"), the *nāma skandha*s existing at that moment do not give rise to successor *nāma skandha*s. Does this mean that the *arhat* is annihilated—that nirvāna means the utter extinction of the enlightened person? No. There is no such thing as the *arhat*, so it lacks meaning to say that the *arhat* is annihilated. And for exactly the same reason, it lacks meaning to say that the *arhat* attains an ineffable state after death.

3.2 Is Nirvāna What the Punctualist Says It Is?

So it is possible to say meaningful things about nirvāna. Buddhists claim that nirvāna is the supremely valuable state that everyone ought to seek. Since we now know that nirvāna is describable, and we want to know whether Buddhists are right to make such a big deal of it, we can ask: What would it be like? In particular, what would it be like to know that there is no self and that "I" is just a convenient designator, that strictly speaking there is no such thing as the enduring person?[2] Parfit says that coming to believe a reductionist view of persons made him less concerned about the rest of his life. This suggests that the enlightened person takes no care for what tomorrow will bring. Perhaps this is because they know that whatever it does bring, it will be someone else who receives it. Is this what cessation with remainder, being enlightened but still alive, is like? Is the *arhat* someone who lives wholly in the present moment? This is a popular interpretation of Buddhist nirvāna. And it sounds like it might be fun. But it is also a mistake. As we saw earlier (in Chapter 1, §3), this Punctualist view is a form of annihilationism. And annihilationism, we know, is one of the two extreme views about our existence that the Buddha says should be rejected in favor of his middle path.

At this point, though, you might wonder whether this can be right. Suppose it's true that there is no enduring self to make me the same person from one stage in my life to the next (or from one life to the next). When I get ready for bed tonight, should I brush my teeth and floss? Brushing my teeth is tedious, and sometimes flossing hurts. So why should I do it? Certainly not for any benefit that these present *skandha*s get out of it. If there's any benefit in doing it, that benefit accrues to the future *skandha*s that avoid the pain of tooth decay and gum disease. And we now know that those future *skandha*s are distinct from these present *skandha*s. So why should these present ones make this sacrifice on behalf of those future ones? Why shouldn't they just

2. More specifically, what would it be like to be an *arhat*, someone who has become enlightened by following the path laid out by a buddha? The Buddhist tradition holds that becoming a buddha takes an immense amount of effort expended over very many lives. So it would be natural to hold that conceiving of what it would be like to be a buddha would be very difficult for most people. But this need not be so with the life of an *arhat*.

appreciate the present for what it is and not worry about the future? Why isn't Punctualism the right conclusion to draw from the reductionist view of persons?

Punctualism is the view that since there is no self, and the parts of the person are all impermanent, the true "I" doesn't last very long: perhaps a day or a week, but maybe just an instant. Since they think this is the truth about us, Punctualists hold we should stop putting so much effort into worrying about the future. Once we do this, they think we will learn to truly appreciate the here and now just as it is. We'll learn to live in the present, and our lives will be fuller and richer for it. But let's think about what the Punctualist says is the truth about us. They say,

> P: The "I" is something that exists only as long as a particular set of skandhas lasts.

Now each of us has a special concern for ourselves. We all take a special interest in our own welfare. And the "I" represents what it is that we identify with. To say that something is part of the "I" is to say that it is one of the things whose welfare I should be concerned about. This is why P has the consequence that we should only be concerned about the present moment. But in what way is P supposed to be true? Is it ultimately true? No. What the Punctualist says we should identify with is the whole consisting of the skandhas that exist together at present: these present body parts and these present thoughts and feelings. This "I" of theirs is a whole. It is not the same whole as the whole that we call a "person." That whole is a causal series of sets of skandhas. The whole that the Punctualist says we should identify with is just one set of skandhas—the ones existing together right now—and not the series made up of a succession of such sets. Still, it is a whole. And wholes are mere conceptual fictions. Since P contains a reference to a whole, it could not be ultimately true. (Nor could it be ultimately false.)

So could P be conventionally true? Remember that for a statement to be conventionally true, it must reliably lead to successful practice. Which way of thinking of ourselves leads to greater success: as things that last for just a very short while, or as persons, things that last at least a lifetime? To answer this question, we need to decide what counts as success in practice. And, of course, different people have different ideas as to what constitutes success. But this is only because of individual differences in how people obtain pleasure and happiness. Surely everyone could agree that successful practice is practice that brings about more pleasure and happiness and less pain and suffering.[3] That makes it quite clear which statement is conventionally true. There is greater overall pleasure and happiness, and less overall pain and suffering, when we think of ourselves as persons than when we think of ourselves in the Punctualist way. Because these present *skandhas* identify with future *skandhas* in the causal series, they brush and floss. And that means less tooth decay and gum disease. If we were to follow the Punctualist's advice, there would be more of this sort of pain and suffering. There would also be less pleasure and happiness. So P is conventionally false. As Nāgasena said, the conventional truth is that we are persons. This is conventionally true because it is ultimately true that these present *skandhas* are the cause of the future *skandhas* in this series. So what these *skandhas* do will affect the welfare of those future *skandhas*. This is why thinking of ourselves as persons results in greater overall welfare.

So Punctualism is not the right way to understand Buddhist nirvāna. Still, someone might try to defend Punctualism against the argument we have just looked at. They might say that this argument

---

3. Objection: there are times when we aim at more rather than less pain, as when someone goes through a hard workout. Reply: the point of working out is not to experience the pain that comes from strenuous exercise. The point is to enjoy the benefits that the workout produces. These may include good health, which amounts to less pain in the long run. These may also include the pleasure that comes with the sense that one has overcome a difficult obstacle. If strenuous exercise only produced pain and no benefits, then most likely no one would ever voluntarily work out.

wrongly defines success as achieving more pleasure and less pain now and in the future. Instead, success should be defined as achieving more present pleasure and less present pain. Future pleasure and pain should not be included in our calculations. The Punctualist would say this is because future pleasure and pain mean nothing to the present "I." Only present pleasure and pain should be counted since those are the only feelings that *this* "I" has. Future pleasure and pain are felt by another "I." And when we define success in this way, P turns out to be conventionally true. If we think of ourselves as persons, then we will brush and floss. At best, this results in present feelings of indifference. There are much better ways to maximize present pleasure and minimize present pain.

Does this objection succeed? You be the judge. But here are some things to consider. The argument in question is for the conclusion that P is conventionally false. The Punctualist objection to this argument is that it begs the question by assuming that future pleasure and pain should count in determining whether a theory is conventionally true or false.[4] But the Buddhist could respond that it would be equally question-begging to assume that only present pleasure and pain should count. Obviously, some neutral standpoint is called for here. Can one be found? What would it look like? (In trying to answer this question you might want to look for clues in the argument of the Mahāyāna philosopher Śāntideva discussed in §4.)

---

4. Begging the question is the fallacy committed when an argument smuggles its conclusion into one of its premises. Here is a stock example: "Of course God exists. It says so in the sacred texts. And everything in the sacred texts is true since it is the word of God." This argument begs the question by including a premise, "the sacred texts are the word of God," that presupposes the truth of the conclusion, "God exists." It is fallacious because you can't prove that the conclusion "God exists" is true by using evidence that already assumes it is true. The fallacy is called "begging the question" because the argument *begs* you to accept its answer to the *question* whether God exists without doing any of the *work* arguments are supposed to do—presenting supporting evidence. And begging is asking for something one hasn't worked for.

3.3 What Nirvāna Might Be Like

We have now ruled out two views about what nirvāna might be like: the view that it is ineffable, and the Punctualist view that it means living wholly in the present. Is there anything positive we can say? By now, it should be clear why enlightenment brings about the cessation of existential suffering. In effect, the Buddhist is saying we experience such suffering because we take too seriously the useful fiction of the person. We experience existential suffering when the fact of our transitoriness makes us question the possibility of meaning and value in our lives. But how did I come to think that my life might have meaning and value? This may seem to be part of what it means to think of oneself as a person. A person is just a useful fiction, though, like "the average college student." We wouldn't make the mistake of searching for the meaning of the life of a statistical fiction like that. So when we feel despair over the seeming pointlessness of our own lives, this is because of a fundamental error in our view of what we are. This might be what Parfit meant when he said that accepting the reductionist view of persons made him less concerned about the rest of his life: that the fact of my mortality no longer inspires existential dread.

To see the Buddhist's point here, it might be useful to consider how we go about socializing small children. As adults, we automatically think of ourselves as persons, so we naturally assume that we always thought this way. But the experience of child-rearing tells us differently. Much of the effort expended in raising a child goes into getting the child to think of itself as a person. That is, the child must learn to identify with ("appropriate") the past and future stages in the causal series of *skandha*s. Take food issues, for instance. Eating healthy foods does not always bring immediate pleasure. But telling the recalcitrant child that eating these foods will promote long-term health has little effect. This isn't necessarily because the child doesn't believe what they are told. It's because the child doesn't identify with the healthy adult it will become if it eats the right food. Its basic attitude is, "Why eat something now that doesn't taste good just for the sake of someone who doesn't even exist? Why should I care about what happens to them?" Likewise, when the child is punished for a past misdeed. Until the child has learned to identify with those past *skandha*s, the child will see this as just the gratuitous infliction of pain by the adult doing the punishing: "Why make me suffer for something somebody else did?" Coming to see themselves as a person is not an easy lesson for the child to learn. We try to make it easier, though, by getting the child to think of their life as a story they get to write. To become a person involves learning to make present sacrifices for the sake of future welfare. The child learns to do this by learning to think of its present choices as having meaning for the future. It learns to think of its life as a kind of narrative. And it learns to think of itself as the central figure in that narrative. Because we learned those lessons well, we expect our lives to have value and significance.

Notice that the Buddhist is not recommending that we become like that small child. The lesson the child learns is important. It leads to there being less overall pain and suffering in the world. It is conventionally true that we are persons. The difficulty the Buddhist is pointing out comes from the way in which we learned that lesson. We learned it by coming to think of ourselves as characters in a drama, figures whose present actions have meaning for the future of the story. And this bit of useful myth-making is what sets the stage for existential suffering. What we need to do is unlearn the myth but continue in the practice. I should continue to identify with the past and future stages of this causal series. But I should not do so because I think of myself as the hero of the story that is my life. I should do so because this is a way of bringing about more pleasure and less pain in the world. Because I feel special concern for the future elements in the series, I brush and floss. And so there is less pain. Because I take responsibility for the past elements in the series, I acknowledge past mistakes and avoid repeating them. And so there is less pain. In one respect, the enlightened person's life is just like ours. We all identify with the past and future stages of the causal series. And we try to brush and floss. The difference is that the enlightened person does so without leaning on the crutch of a self that confers meaning and value on the events of a life. The enlightened person avoids the pain of tooth decay, just like the rest of us. But the enlightened person also avoids existential suffering.

One common reaction to this account of nirvāna is to find it hugely depressing. This often stems from the sense that the Buddhist account robs life of all meaning. If the events in my life don't fit into some larger scheme, then what's the point? It's little consolation to be told that the sense that our lives each have their own unique purpose always was just an illusion. But according to the Buddhist, this reaction rests on a still deeper mistake. For the lack of ultimate meaning to be grounds for depression, there must exist a subject for whom meaninglessness is a source of despair. When the Buddhist denies that our lives have meaning, it is not because they hold that our lives are inherently meaningless. It is rather because they hold that meaning requires something that does not ultimately exist, the subject for whom events in a life can have meaning. If there is no such subject—if there is no self—then there is equally no subject whose life can lack all meaning. There is no one whose life either has or lacks meaning. There is just the life.

This last point helps us see how there just might be some truth to the claim that being enlightened means living in the here and now. We saw that being enlightened does not mean having no concern for the future consequences of my present actions. But it is one thing to consider tomorrow's hangover when deciding how much beer to drink tonight. It is another to see that decision as defining who I am. It can be burdensome to see each event in my life as having meaning for my identity. This can detract from our appreciation of the present. And it can make bad experiences worse. Being sick or injured is painful. But in addition to the pain itself, there is the anxiety that comes from wondering what this pain says about who I am and where I am going. When the enlightened person is sick or injured, they will seek the appropriate medical help to relieve their pain. But they will not experience the suffering we ordinarily feel in those circumstances. They are liberated from the burdens that come with the sense of a self. Perhaps this is why, in Buddhist art, an enlightened person such as a buddha is often depicted with a serene half-smile on their face.

3.4 Grounding Moral Obligation

At this point, we will move on to the second part of our investigation of Buddhist ethics. We have been looking at the consequences of non-self for the part of ethics concerned with how we should live our own lives—with why we should seek nirvāna. We will now examine how the doctrine of non-self affects our obligations toward others. What moral consequences might follow from the person's being a mere conceptual fiction? If the enlightened person is someone who knows this to be true, how would this affect their moral conduct? In the passage we quoted earlier, Parfit said that coming to accept the reductionist view of persons led him to be less concerned about the rest of his life and more concerned about the lives of others. We have seen how Buddhists could agree with the first part of this statement. Do they also agree with the second? Does enlightenment lead to moral improvement?

If we think of Buddhism as a religion, we will certainly expect Buddhists to have much to say about morality. Religions are widely seen as a major source of moral training for their adherents. This expectation will not be disappointed. Buddhist literature is rife with lists of virtues that should be cultivated and vices that should be abandoned, uplifting stories of moral exemplars, cautionary tales about the sad fates of people who went astray, and the like. But many people see a much tighter connection between religion and morality. They think of religion as belief in a transcendent power and morality as a set of rules specifying acceptable treatment of others. The connection they see is that the rules are commands of the higher power. On this view, religious faith is actually required if one is to be moral. Only belief in God, it is thought, will move one to obey the moral law when temptation urges otherwise. But no Buddhist would accept this picture. Since Buddhism is atheist (in the sense discussed in §2 of the Introduction), Buddhists will not think of moral rules as divine commands. What makes it wrong to take another's property, for instance, cannot be that the Buddha forbids it.[5] So can Buddhism actually provide a foundation for morality? Can it give a satisfactory answer to the question of why I should be moral?

In Plato's dialogue *Republic*, this question is posed in a particularly forceful way. Suppose there were a ring that made one invisible. Would someone with such a ring not use it to their own advantage even when doing so meant violating the commonly accepted moral rules? If you could steal from a bank in a way that was guaranteed to be undetectable, would you? The problem here is not one of moral ignorance. We know that stealing is wrong. The problem is one of moral motivation: Why should I be moral? A theist may have a ready answer to this question. While a magic ring might make us invisible to other humans, God would see us and punish us for our sin. A Buddhist cannot say this. Nor can they say we should be moral out of love of our creator. Buddhists do not believe there is a being who created us. So what can the Buddhist say? Why, according to the Buddhist, should we be moral?

The Buddhist answer has three layers. Each layer answers the question of moral motivation in a way that is responsive to the abilities of people at a certain stage on the path to nirvāna. The first answer is that we should obey the moral rules because they reflect the karmic causal laws. Stealing, for instance, is motivated by a desire that causes

---

5. As Plato pointed out in *Euthyphro*, calling moral rules divine commands simply forestalls answering the question why they should be followed. If theft is wrong because God commands us not to do it, we can always ask why God wants us not to steal. Is this purely arbitrary? Or is there some feature of theft and other immoral acts that explains why God forbids them? If the latter, then what makes them wrong is not that they violate God's commands. It is this wrong-making feature, whatever it is, that led God to forbid them.

bad karmic fruit, such as rebirth as a *preta*. Acts of benevolence toward strangers, on the other hand, are motivated by desires that cause good karmic fruit, such as rebirth as a god or a high-status human. Since I would much rather be reborn as a high-status human than as a *preta*, it is to my advantage to refrain from stealing and to practice benevolence toward strangers. This answer will obviously satisfy only those who accept the doctrine of karma and rebirth. More importantly, though, it works only for those whose primary aim in life is to attain pleasure and happiness. These are not people who are actively seeking nirvāna. We said above that each layer represents a teaching designed for those who have reached a certain point on the path to nirvāna. How can such people be said to be on the path? Does this teaching contribute to anyone's progress toward nirvāna?

The answer to this question takes us into the second layer. The Buddha speaks of three poisons (*kleśas*), factors that account for our remaining bound in samsāra. The three are greed, hatred, and delusion. These factors have the interesting property of being self-perpetuating. This is because the three poisons tend to motivate certain sorts of actions, and these actions, in turn, tend to reinforce the three poisons. Here "delusion" refers to ignorance of the three characteristics (impermanence, suffering, and non-self). Greed and hatred clearly presuppose such ignorance, particularly ignorance of non-self. Greed and hatred also lead us to act in ways that reinforce our ignorance, thus setting the stage for further bouts of greed and hatred. When my greed leads me to take something that is not mine, for instance, I am reinforcing the belief that there is an "I" that can be made better off through what it possesses. The result is a kind of feedback loop that is supposed to explain why the cycle of rebirths has gone on for so long. The eightfold path that the Buddha taught (see Chapter 1, §3) is meant to help us break out of this loop. You will recall that three of the eight factors in this path—right speech, right conduct, and right livelihood—represent the basic moral virtues that lay followers of the Buddha are to cultivate. Right conduct, for instance, includes such things as habitually refraining from stealing, while right speech includes the virtue of honesty. Why are these included in the path to nirvāna? Not because they generate pleasant karmic fruits. Instead, it is because such virtues help counteract the three poisons. A certain kind of moral training is a necessary prerequisite for attaining the kind of insight that leads to nirvāna.

The answer of the first layer said we should be moral because doing so will lead to a pleasant rebirth. The answer of the second layer says we should be moral because doing so is part of the training necessary for attaining nirvāna. In order to counteract the three poisons, we must develop habits that serve as antidotes to greed, hatred, and delusion. The virtue of honesty, for instance, will make us more likely to accept the truth about ourselves. And the virtue of habitually refraining from taking what is not ours will help diminish our desire for possessions. Of course, the three poisons still have ample scope in the life of the conventionally virtuous person. I might never steal, and yet I might still covet those things I cannot rightfully attain. I might feel righteous anger at those not as morally upstanding as I take myself to be. But the conventional morality that is inculcated through belief in karma and rebirth is just an early stage of the path. The point of these moral practices is to counteract the three poisons just enough to make it possible to renounce the householder's existence and become a monk or nun. With entry into the Buddhist monastic order comes a whole new set of moral practices designed to help extinguish the three poisons. One is, for instance, required to be celibate, and the only possessions traditionally allowed the monk or nun are one's robes and an alms bowl. There are meditational exercises designed to counteract sensual desire, which is an especially powerful form of greed. There are exercises designed to help one cultivate equanimity and loving-kindness toward all, thereby curbing our tendency toward anger. The claim is that by following this regime of retraining our emotional habits, we will ultimately become able to fully grasp the truth about ourselves—that there is no self—and thus attain nirvāna.

Suppose this is right. Then the person who seeks nirvāna will know not to engage in immoral conduct. This is not because nirvāna is a reward for those who are morally pure. It is rather because immoral conduct stems from motives that interfere with the liberating insight of non-self. But what about the person who has attained nirvāna? Why should they be moral? Not because doing so will help them attain nirvāna. They have already attained it. Is there anything about enlightenment that could constitute a source of moral motivation? We have reached the third layer. What we will find here is an argument for the obligation to be benevolent: whenever we are able to prevent others from experiencing pain or suffering, we must do so. So to the extent that being moral consists in giving equal consideration to the welfare of others, this can be seen as an argument for an obligation to be moral. The immorality of stealing, for instance, can be explained by the fact that the thief intends to benefit while causing others pain. To be moral is to give the welfare of others no less intrinsic weight than one gives one's own welfare. Benevolence could be said to be the soul of morality. So an argument for the obligation to be benevolent would serve to answer the question of why I should be moral.

This argument will not claim that being moral is a means to some other end we might want, such as good rebirth or nirvāna. Instead, it will claim that if we properly understand what it is that we say we want, we will see that we must want to promote the welfare of others. The key to this proper understanding is, of course, becoming enlightened. The argument will claim that once we fully grasp the truth of non-self, we will see that there is no reason to prefer our own welfare over that of others. And since everyone already acknowledges that they ought to promote their own welfare, it follows that anyone who is enlightened must acknowledge an obligation to promote the welfare of others as well. But the obligation that it argues for does not apply just to the enlightened. It applies to all of us if it is true that there is no self.

The argument begins by comparing our usual attitude toward the suffering of others with our attitude toward our own possible future suffering. It uses the assumption of karma and rebirth and describes the attitude one might take toward one's next life.

> 97. If one says that the suffering of other persons does not harm me, hence efforts need not be made to prevent it,
> Then since the suffering of future bodies does not harm me, why should efforts be made?
> 98. "It will also be just me then as well" is a mistaken construction,
> For it is one thing that dies and something else entirely that is born.
> 99. If it is thought that the suffering to be prevented is just one's own,
> Pain in the foot is not that of the hand. Why should the one protect the other?
> 100. If it is objected that while that [partiality with respect to one's own suffering] is mistaken, it results from the sense of "I,"
> That is wrong, and this way of thinking of oneself and the other is to be abandoned to the best of one's ability.
> 101. The series and the collection, like a queue, an army and so on, are unreal.
> The one who owns the suffering does not exist. Therefore, whose will it be?
> 102. All sufferings are ownerless because all are devoid of distinction [between "mine" and "other"].
> Because it is suffering, it is to be prevented; how can any limitation be imposed?
> 103. Why then is suffering to be prevented? Because it is agreed upon without exception by all [that it is].
> Thus if it is to be prevented, then indeed all of it is to be prevented; if not, then one's own case is just like that of other persons. (BCA VIII.97–103)[6]

---

6. The author of this argument, Śāntideva, belongs to the Madhyamaka school of Mahāyāna Buddhism, a school that we will briefly examine in Chapter 4. Madhyamaka views differ from those of other Buddhist philosophical schools. But the argument presented here does not involve any controversial premises.

The first two verses are discussing the fact that someone who believes in karma and rebirth would do what they could to prevent being reborn with a very painful body. We think this is perfectly sensible since if you believe in rebirth, then you think the person with that painful body will be you. The point being made in the verses is that the *skandha*s constituting the future person with the painful body are not the *skandha*s that make up me now. Of course, not everyone believes in rebirth. But as we saw in the last chapter, we could say the same thing about the *skandha*s making up a person at one stage of life and the *skandha*s constituting that person later in life. So we could say the same thing about the person brushing their teeth and the person whose cavities are thereby prevented. Consequently, we could change the second half of verse 98 to "It is one set of teeth that are brushed and quite another whose cavities are prevented."

Verse 99 considers the case where my hand removes a splinter from my foot. We think this is equally sensible since hand and foot are both parts of, so I am acting to stop my own suffering. The verse makes the point that hand and foot are nonetheless distinct things. So we now have two cases where we think it is sensible to prevent pain, yet strictly speaking, it is one thing that has the pain and something else that acts to prevent it. Yet, we also think it is perfectly reasonable for each of us to take a special interest in our own welfare. We think that if someone else's suffering won't affect us in any way, then we have no obligation to do anything about it. While we may think it would be very nice to help others, we believe it would not be irrational to attend to only our own pain and not that of others. The rest of the passage discusses the apparent conflict between this common attitude and the two cases discussed in the first three verses. We could put all of this as follows:

1. Suppose that we are each obligated to prevent only our own suffering.

2. In the case of one's own future suffering, it is one set of *skandha*s that does the preventing for the benefit of another set that has the suffering.

3. In the case of one's own present suffering, it is one part that does the preventing for the benefit of another part that has the suffering.

4. The sense of "I" that leads one to call future *skandha*s and distinct present *skandha*s "me" is a conceptual fiction.

5. Hence it cannot be ultimately true that some suffering is one's own and some suffering is that of others.

6. Hence the claim that we are obligated to prevent only our own suffering lacks ultimate grounding.

7. Hence either there is an obligation to prevent suffering regardless of when or where it occurs, or else there is no obligation to prevent any suffering.

8. But everyone agrees that at least some suffering should be prevented (namely one's own).

Conclusion: there is an obligation to prevent suffering regardless of when or where it occurs.

What this argument in effect does is accuse us of irrationality if we think it's justifiable to be concerned about our own pain and not be equally concerned about the pain of other people. The crucial premise is (4). This is where non-self gets brought in. It claims that there is no ultimate fact that could back up our discriminating between our own pain and that of others. Suppose there is no self. If wholes are also unreal, then hand and foot cannot be parts of one whole, my body. This is likened to the case of an army. When the helicopter pilot evacuates the wounded soldier, it is one thing that acts on another. If wholes are unreal, then the present body and the future body cannot be stages of one thing, me. This is likened to the case of a queue. The line for a movie is made up of different people at 9:00 and 9:15. The army and the movie queue are just useful fictions. There are really just the parts making them up. So, as (6) concludes, there are no ultimate facts that could explain on the one hand why I should take that splinter out of my foot and I should brush and floss, but why, on the other hand, I need not have the same concern for preventing the suffering of others. Premise (7) then points out that there are two remaining options: that suffering should be prevented regardless of "whose" it is or that absolutely nothing matters. It might be consistent of me to do nothing to prevent any pain anywhere—my own or that of others. But that would be insane. Pain and suffering are bad, which means that they are to be prevented. So the obligation that I already acknowledge to prevent my own pain extends equally to the suffering of others. Once I overcome the illusion of a self, I will see that my desire to prevent my own pain is really just a desire to prevent pain, period.

We know that Buddhists deny the existence of a self. Many people also know that Buddhists claim an enlightened person will necessarily be benevolent.[7] It might be tempting to see these two things as connected in the following way: "If I have no self, then you and I aren't really distinct people, we are really one, so I should be just as concerned about your welfare as I am about my own." But this is not what the Buddhist is saying. The trouble comes with the "we are really one." There are Indian philosophers who actually say something like this. But they are not Buddhists; they belong to the orthodox school called Advaita Vedānta. Unlike the Buddhists, they hold that there is a self. But unlike other orthodox Indian philosophers, they hold that there really is just one self. So they would say that what we think of as distinct persons really aren't distinct. The Buddhist argument we just

---

7. It is actually compassion, not benevolence, which Buddhists discuss. But the difference may not matter for our purposes. In Mahāyāna Buddhism it is claimed that the bodhisattva (an enlightened person who desists from entering into final nirvāna) is filled with compassion toward all sentient beings. And since the text from which our argument is taken is a Mahāyāna text, you might suspect that this argument only applies to Mahāyāna, not to Early Buddhism and Abhidharma. But Abhidharma also holds that enlightened persons will feel compassion toward others. Moreover, the premises of our argument would be acceptable to any Buddhist.

looked at agrees that we are not really distinct persons. But what Buddhists deny is not the distinctness. They deny that there are persons. They deny that there are those things that could be either many or else really one. The Advaitin and the Buddhist can both argue for the same conclusion—that we should show equal concern for the welfare of all. But they argue for it in very different ways.

Does the Buddhist argument really work? If so, it would do something that many people think can't be done: provide a rational, non-theistic foundation for morality. But here is one question to consider. In (6), it is concluded from (4) and (5) that there is no ultimate ground for the claim that we are obligated to prevent only our own suffering. Is this right? We saw (in Chapter 2) how the Buddhist defends (4). And if (4) is true, then (5) must be as well. Ultimately there is just suffering, not the person who has it. But suffering only occurs together with other *skandha*s as part of a causal series of *skandha*s. Remember that while persons are not ultimately real, it is conventionally true that we are persons. And this conventional truth is grounded in the ultimate existence of a causal series of *skandha*s. Because these *skandha*s were caused by those earlier ones, it is conventionally true that it's my own fault if I have cavities—I am the same person as the one who didn't brush regularly. All of this we already knew. But here is another point that has not yet come up: there are many distinct causal series. These can be distinguished by virtue of where the effects show up. The persistent refusal to brush in this series will not cause cavities in another causal series, only in this one. Might this not explain why we conveniently designate the one series as "me" and the other as "you"? Might this not be the ultimate truth that makes it conventionally true that we are distinct persons? In this case perhaps there is some ultimate ground for the claim that we are obligated to prevent only our own suffering. Perhaps (6) does not follow from (4) and (5). Perhaps (6) is false.

In philosophy we often come across arguments that look convincing but make claims that seem too strong to be plausible. The

Buddhist argument for benevolence might be an example. If we have understood and accepted the doctrine of non-self, the argument seems perfectly simple and straightforward. But when we reflect on what it purports to prove, it starts to seem like it might be too good to be true. Philosophers in the Western tradition have long sought to establish a rational obligation to be moral, with little success to show for their efforts. Could it really be this easy? The study of philosophy may make us skeptical. This is why, when we encounter a plausible-seeming argument for a surprising conclusion, we need to be careful. We need to test the argument by looking for hidden flaws: either false premises or holes in the reasoning. We need to adopt the stance of someone raising objections to the argument, looking for ways to show that the argument does not really prove its conclusion. But our work is not over once we've found an objection. Sometimes objections are not as good as they initially seem. So we need to lay out the objection clearly and carefully. And then, we need to adopt the stance of someone defending the argument against that objection. Is there anything they can say that shows the argument does not really have the problem the opponent alleges it has? In the case of the Buddhist argument for benevolence, we sketched a strategy for raising an objection in the preceding paragraph. But this was just a sketch. Now the details need to be filled in more carefully. Once this is done, you should ask yourself what the Buddhist could say in response. If you have spelled out the objection with sufficient care, you may find there are still moves the Buddhist can make. Or perhaps not. What is important is that the effort be made. Philosophical arguments can be very persuasive. But we want to be sure we are not persuaded for the wrong reasons. This is why, when we encounter such an argument, we put it to the test. First, we try to understand it, then we put ourselves in the position of an opponent and look for objections, then we see how those objections might be replied to. If you do this with the Buddhist argument for benevolence, you may end up more confident that the final conclusion you reach is based on good reasons.

3.5 Does a Causal Series of Sets of *Skandha*s Have Free Will?

Ethics is all about right and wrong, about how to tell when someone does something deserving praise or blame. As such, it concerns the actions of those we consider responsible agents. Here is something that may have been bothering you. The only sorts of things that could be responsible agents are persons, and Buddhists say that a person is really just a causal series of sets of *skandha*s. This means that everything a "person" does is actually the effect of prior causes. And if all my actions are causally determined, how can I be responsible for any of them? Doesn't responsibility require that what one does is the result of a free choice to do this rather than that? If my choosing to do this rather than that is itself the effect of prior causes, how can it be free?

These are some of the questions that come up in the so-called free will debate in philosophy. It's called this because one side of the debate holds that if the will is caused, then it cannot be free, and free will is required for moral responsibility. The other side agrees that if everything is caused, then the will couldn't be "free" in the sense of being something that chooses without being influenced by what came before. But this other side denies that the will's being "free" in this sense is required for moral responsibility. They say that I can still be held accountable for an action even if my choosing to do it was caused by earlier events. They believe that causal determinism (the view that every event is caused) is compatible with moral responsibility.

This is a debate that has gone on for a long time in Western philosophy. But there is nothing like this debate in Indian philosophy. (Scholars of the Chinese philosophical tradition say it didn't come up there either.) So Buddhist philosophers of classical India haven't given an answer to a question that may have been bothering you. But the scholars studying Buddhist philosophy today are familiar with the "free will" debate and have begun to think about what a Buddhist philosopher might say about it. A variety of different views have emerged from these discussions. Here is one that makes use of the distinction between the conventional truth and the ultimate truth about the things we call persons.

Suppose that while you are asleep, I take all the money from your wallet and use it to party all night. You wake up the next morning, find your wallet empty, hear about my exploits, and tell me I'm guilty of stealing, something we agree is wrong. I deny your accusation, but my only defense is that the *skandha*s that chose to take the money were caused to be the way they were by earlier *skandha*s, which were in turn caused by yet earlier *skandha*s, in a causal series that stretches back to before I was born. Since we agree that an event that is causally determined by earlier conditions has to happen, and we also agree that I can't be held responsible for how things were before I was even born, I say it follows that I'm not responsible for what happened. I may agree that it's too bad you're now broke, but I cannot be blamed. Since guilt requires responsibility, I'm not guilty of stealing.

You shouldn't be convinced by my reasoning, but why not? Well, notice that in order to assess my responsibility for the act of taking the money, we need to look at not just the *skandha*s at the moment my hand touched your wallet, but also the *skandha*s at the time I was thinking about what to do and how to do it. I deliberated about my action and chose to do it based on those deliberations. And in order to know if those deliberations were conducted in the right way (the way that would make me responsible), we will need to look at still earlier *skandha*s that made the deliberation events go the way they did. And so on. We need, in other words, to look not just at the *skandha*s that were present at the time of the act but at the causal series of distinct *skandha*s that culminated in those *skandha*s. That's what takes me back to before I was born—and so to something we all agree I can't be held responsible for. But now remember Milinda's Principle (Chapter 2, §7) and Nāgasena's response. Milinda thought that different *skandha*s must make for different persons, so that the infant Milinda and the adult Milinda are two different people. Nāgasena replied that the infant *skandha*s and the adult *skandha*s are neither the same person nor are they different persons. This is because the things we say about *skandha*s are ultimately true, whereas talk about persons can only be conventionally true. What's ultimately true explains why certain things are conventionally true. But it's a mistake to suppose that conventionally true statements could themselves be ultimately true or ultimately false. What if the Buddhist could show that the same holds with respect to judgments of responsibility?

The idea would be this: judgments of responsibility are judgments about persons. Only a person can have the property of being responsible for doing something, of deserving praise or blame for an action. Since persons are wholes made of parts, they are not ultimately real. So it cannot make sense to say that things that are ultimately real, like sets of *skandha*s, are responsible for some action. Nor that they are not responsible either. Judgments of responsibility can only make sense at the level of conventional truth (just as judgments of personal identity can only be conventionally true or false). There are, though, certain conditions that make it be either conventionally true or conventionally false that a person is responsible for an action. If I thought about what I was doing when I took the cash from your wallet, if I deliberated about the options and considered their consequences, and then decided to act based on the outcome of my deliberations, then we would call me responsible for what I did. And those events can be described in terms of facts about the causal series of *skandha*s that make up this "me." If the decisive intention causing the hand motion was caused by certain sorts of awareness events triggered by certain sorts of dispositions and certain memory traces, then it's conventionally true that I am responsible. If not, then it is conventionally true that I am not responsible. The fact that the ultimate events are all parts of a causal series is neither here nor there when it comes to judgments of responsibility. Ultimate facts can make it conventionally true or conventionally false that I am responsible for what happened. All the ultimate facts involve events that occur in accordance with causal determinism. But the causal determinism that holds at the ultimate level is perfectly compatible with its being conventionally true that I am guilty of stealing. If the sequence of *skandhas* constitutes what we consider a reasoned deliberation, then I am responsible. You'd be right to call me a thief.

Does this strategy work? Can the Buddhist use it to reconcile their determinism about the *skandhas* with their view that moral judgments can be true or false? That's for you to decide. If you think not, then there are other approaches that a Buddhist might take to try to resolve the difficulty. And since it is only recently that this question has been raised, it's not even yet clear that there is only one approach a Buddhist philosopher might take, or for that matter, that any approach can succeed. One thing we can take away from this, though, is that the philosophical tradition that grew out of the Buddha's teachings is not a closed book. We have more to say about this in the next chapter.

Some Key Points of This Chapter

- The Buddha rejected all four possible descriptions of nirvāna because each falsely presupposes that it is the state of a person (ultimately there are no persons).

- Buddhist enlightenment is not a mere matter of "living in the moment," since the enlightened person does consider the consequences of present choices for future parts of the causal series of *skandhas*.

- Because enlightened persons understand the sense of self to be illusory, they are motivated to strive to prevent suffering regardless of where it occurs, whether "mine" or "someone else's."

- Since Buddhists claim that all the events in the life of a person are causally determined by prior events, they may need some response to the objection that this means no one is ever responsible for their actions; one possible response involves distinguishing between what is ultimately true—that these *skandhas* were caused by earlier *skandhas*—and what is conventionally true—that the person freely chose to do the deed.

For Further Reading

Two different views of the overall character of Buddhist ethics, including surveys of Buddhist views on a variety of ethical questions, are to be found in: (1) Christopher Gowans, *Buddhist Moral Philosophy: An Introduction* (New York: Routledge, 2016); and in (2) Charles Goodman, *Consequences of Compassion* (New York: Oxford University Press, 2009).

For a very different reading of the argument for benevolence, see Paul Williams, *Altruism and Reality: Studies in the Philosophy of the Bodhicāryāvatāra* (Richmond, UK: Curzon Press, 1998). See in addition some of the essays in The Cowherds, eds., *Moonpaths* (New York: Oxford University Press, 2016), which also contains a complete translation of Śāntideva's argument for benevolence together with a prose commentary.

For a discussion of the nature of altruism and its treatment in Buddhist ethics and utilitarianism, see the chapter entitled "The Emotions of Altruism, East and West," in Joel Kupperman, *Learning from Asian Philosophy* (New York: Oxford University Press, 1999), pp. 145–55.

Derek Parfit's discussion of the ethical consequences of reductionism about persons is contained in Chapters 14 and 15 of his *Reasons and Persons* (Oxford: Oxford University Press, 1984). There is now a substantial critical literature on his position. Some of the best essays are collected in: Jonathan Dancy, ed., *Reading Parfit* (Oxford: Basil Blackwell, 1997). A more recent collection is Andrea Sauchelli, ed., *Derek Parfit's Reasons and Persons* (London: Routledge, 2020).

A collection of original papers on the problem of determinism and moral responsibility in Buddhism is found in: Rick Repetti, ed., *Buddhist Perspectives on Free Will: Agentless Agency?* (London: Routledge, 2016).

Chapter Four

The Rest of the Story

We now have a basic idea of what Buddhist philosophy looked like at the beginning of the Common Era. So even if the ideas we've discussed so far were not actually taught by the Buddha (something we may not be able to know), they represent things that later Buddhist philosophers took to be definitive of their tradition. This is how what are considered the Buddha's teachings look when they are taken as philosophy. So how does the rest of the story go? Very differently. Different from what, though? Not from the teachings presented in the preceding chapters. The differences are among what various Buddhist philosophers made of that core stock of theories and issues. In this final chapter, we will look at three very different ways that later Buddhist thinkers built on and developed these central ideas. Our discussion will not be as detailed and systematic as what we have had so far. This is not the place to try to present in any detail the different theories of later Buddhist philosophers and the arguments they gave in support. All we can hope to do here is convey some sense of the rich diversity of views that grew out of what the tradition took as the Buddha's basic teachings.

Here are some of the things that all Buddhist philosophers accept:

- the analysis of suffering, its causes, and how it can be ended;

- non-self and impermanence;

- dependent origination as the key to explaining our false beliefs about non-self, impermanence, and suffering;

- the availability of a path that brings about the cessation of suffering.

As Buddhist philosophers began to systematize and clarify these doctrines and began to debate non-Buddhists concerning their content, they developed some new views, views they thought were at least implicit in the Buddha's teachings and were also rationally defensible. Three of these stand out as important to later developments:

1. Mereological nihilism: the view that only things without parts are strictly speaking or ultimately real;

2. The intrinsic nature criterion: the view that only those things are ultimately real whose nature is not dependent on how other things are at that time;

3. Momentariness: the view that ultimately real entities exist for just a moment, going out of existence immediately after coming into existence.

We've already encountered the first of these (in Chapter 2, §5), but (2) and (3) are new; we'll be explaining them in detail as we proceed. We'll be looking at theories developed by three different Indian Buddhist philosophical schools: Vaibhāṣika, Yogācāra, and Madhyamaka. Each of these schools accepts all three views, in one form or another. Their differences grow out of the different ways they understand (1), (2), and (3), and what they think follows from them. Historically, Vaibhāṣika is the earliest of the three, and the positions of the other two schools develop in response to Vaibhāṣika doctrines. So we will start our investigation with them.

4.1 Mereological Nihilism and the Vaibhāṣika Theory of *Dharma*s As Things with Intrinsic Natures

Vaibhāṣika is one of the schools making up the Abhidharma movement.[1] Abhidharma arose out of efforts to systematize and codify the Buddha's teachings. One result of these efforts is the development of an

---

1. Historians count some eighteen such schools; one of these, Theravāda, is the form of Buddhism practiced today in Sri Lanka and much of Southeast Asia.

argument for mereological nihilism. This position, it will be recalled, is crucial to the Buddhist defense of non-self. For it explains why "I" cannot be the name of the person, if the person is a whole composed of the five kinds of psychophysical elements. Mereological nihilism tells us that strictly speaking there is no such thing as a person, only the elements making up body and mind. But why should we accept mereological nihilism? When we first discussed this doctrine, we called it a kind of ontological bias against wholes as things with parts. And why accept a bias? Vaibhāṣika philosophers responded with what can be called the "Neither Identical nor Distinct" argument for mereological nihilism.

The basic strategy of the "Neither Identical nor Distinct" argument is to look at the two possible ways that a whole like a chariot and its parts (such as the axle, the wheels, etc.) could all be real: either the chariot is identical with the parts, or else it is something separate and distinct. So if a chariot were made up of, say, seventy-five parts, the first option would be saying that there are just seventy-five things where the chariot is, while the second option would say that there are seventy-six. The first option is ruled out on the grounds that a really existing chariot would have different properties than the parts out of which it is made. One can ride a chariot but not on an axle or banner staff, and the chariot would have the property of being one thing, while its parts have the very different property of being seventy-five things. This makes it seem like a chariot would have to be distinct from its parts, something that exists over and above the axle, wheels, and so on. But this option has its difficulties. For instance, distinct physical objects cannot occupy the same space. If your car is completely filling a parking space, mine won't fit there too. So how can a chariot occupy precisely the space where all the parts are if it is just as distinct from them as our two cars are distinct from each other? The argument claims that the best way to think about these things is that "chariot" is just a useful way of talking about all the parts when they are assembled in the right way—that the word is a convenient designator. And to say that words like "chariot" or "person" are convenient designators is to say that strictly speaking, there are no such things as chariots or persons. Anything we think of as real but that is composite is not ultimately real; it is only conventionally real—something that is thought to exist only because of our convention of using a single name for the collection of the parts of which it is composed.

We won't try to evaluate this argument; our job here is just to look at what the consequences would be if the argument is sound. We already know that it would mean the only ultimately real things are simple or impartite. So most of the things we ordinarily think of as real turn out not to be—at least if by "real" we mean how things truly objectively are. To call the chariot a conceptual fiction (to say it is only conventionally real) is to say that its being real depends not only on the objective way the world is but also on our interests and cognitive limitations. It's in our interests to have means of transportation, and it would be hard for us to keep in mind all the different parts. These are subjective facts, facts about us that color our perception of the world. But what are the ultimately real things like, the things that do objectively exist?

Vaibhāṣika philosophers developed an interesting test for something's being ultimately real. The basic idea is this: take something that we think of as real and ask yourself if our name for that sort of thing would still apply "after division and analysis." The "after division" part of the test is easy to apply. When we disassemble a chariot what we are left with—the individual chariot parts—would no longer be considered a chariot. An axle is not a chariot. The same thing goes for trees, mountains, houses, and persons: a leaf is not a tree, a rock is not a mountain, and so on. Trees, mountains, houses, and persons are not ultimately real.

The "after analysis" part of the test is more complicated. To see how it works, consider something we think should survive the "after division" part of the test: a water atom. We need to remember that classical Indian philosophers (like their Western contemporaries)

thought that water was an element and not a compound (two atoms
of hydrogen and one atom of oxygen). Let's suppose, with them, that
no matter how finely you divide up a quantity of water, what you get
is still water—even when you reach the finest possible amount. That
smallest possible particle of water would be an indivisible atom. Since
it is still something we can call "water," it survives the "after division"
part of the test. But what happens when we try to describe our water
atom? Here are some things we might say about it: round, wet, transparent, having a mass of 3×10^{-23} grams, and so on. That we say such
things as that the water atom is wet, round, and so on, means we think
of being wet, round, and so on as qualities of this atom. The "after
analysis" test involves asking if "water atom" would still apply when
we analyze the atom into these individual qualities. And the answer to
this is surely not. We wouldn't call an individual occurrence of roundness or transparency a water atom. If we perceived (through a very
powerful microscope) the occurrence of roundness or transparency,
we might take this as a *sign* that there is a water atom there. But to say
this is to bring out the fact that by "water atom" we mean a *thing* that
has the qualities of being round, transparent, and so on. We would be
taking the occurrence of the roundness as evidence for the presence
of other things. So "water atom" is a many masquerading as a one:
the "thing" itself, plus all the qualities that are supposed to make it a
"water atom" thing.

At this point, you might object that there couldn't be the occurrence of roundness or wetness without there being the thing that is
round or wet. So even if our analysis of the water atom reveals there
to be many different aspects going into its being a water atom, there
is still just one entity there, the "thing" that has the qualities that
make it be a water atom. This is not, then, like the case of the chariot, where the one big thing got broken down into smaller things—an
axle, wheels, and so on. The Vaibhāṣika will respond, though, with a
question: What exactly is this "thing" that is the bearer of the qualities
of being round, transparent, and so on? If you say that it is something

that's round, wet, and so on, they'll reply that you haven't answered their question. You are describing the qualities, but the question was about the "thing" itself, the bearer of those qualities. What this brings out is that this idea of a "thing" such as a water atom may just be a way of tying up in one bundle a bunch of qualities that happen to occur together. It may just be a conceptual fiction. Whenever we encounter occurrences of roundness and wetness, we also encounter occurrences of transparency and a certain mass, and so we have found it convenient to bundle all of them together under one label. We then forget that this label is just a convenience—we mistake it for the name of some real entity, the water atom. The "after analysis" test is meant to remind us that the water atom is like the chariot in being something that "dissolves" when we look more closely, only in this case not dissolving under division but under analysis.

This idea takes some getting used to. Our commonsense picture of the world is organized around the idea of things (philosophers call them "substances") as the bearers of qualities. So much so that we think there can't be an occurrence of wetness without there being a thing that is wet. And the Vaibhāṣika would agree that this way of thinking makes sense when it comes to organizing our experience in a way that helps us get around in the world of daily life. The concept of water as what is wet, colorless, transparent, occurring in spherical droplets, and so on, is a much more convenient way to organize our experience with the watery part of the world: it gives us a single hook on which to hang all the different experiences we have, so that when we encounter one of them we can use that hook to bring up other experiences we can expect to have. But precisely because it's no more than just that useful hook to hang our expectations on, there is no reason to think that the concept corresponds to anything in objective reality. There are no water atoms, ultimately, just occurrences of qualities like wetness.

Particular occurrences of wetness are among the things that remain "after division and analysis." The term for such ultimately real

entities is *dharma*. You will recall from Chapter 2, §2 that the Buddha
used the term *skandha* for his classification of the parts into which persons can be analyzed. The five *skandha*s are the five different kinds
of constituents of persons and other entities: *rūpa*, feeling, perception,
volition, and consciousness. Vaibhāṣika recognizes seventy-five different kinds of *dharmas*, their list being organized around the *skandha*
classification. So an occurrence of wetness would count as a *dharma*
that falls under the category of *rūpa skandha*, while an occurrence of
pleasure would count as another *dharma* falling under the category of
feeling *skandha*. Many texts of Abhidharma schools like Vaibhāṣika
are largely devoted to classifying *dharmas* and discussing their relations among one another. Some people (including some Buddhists)
find these discussions "scholastic" in the bad sense—too concerned
with matters of mere bookkeeping at the expense of more important
spiritual matters. We'll come back to this point later. Right now, the
important question is how you tell whether something really is a *dharma*,
something objectively, ultimately real. What is the test of *dharma*-
hood? We know that a *dharma* will be something the name of which
still applies after "division and analysis." But is there anything positive
we can say about *dharmas*?

The Vaibhāṣika answer is that a *dharma* is something with intrinsic nature or *svabhāva*. The *bhāva* of this Sanskrit compound means
"nature," and the *sva* (related to Latin *sua*, Spanish *si*, French *se*, and
English *self-*) means "its own." So: something whose nature is wholly
its own. The idea is that a *dharma* must be something that is the way
that it is, is the sort of thing it is, independently of the way that other
things around it are. It must be something whose nature does not
depend on the existence of other things. One way to understand this
test for *dharma*-hood or ultimate reality is to ask whether the entity
in question could exist as the sort of thing that it is if it were the only
thing in the universe at that moment. A chariot clearly flunks this test.
There can't be a chariot unless there are the two wheels, the axle,
and so on. There likewise can't be a water atom unless there are the

occurrences of wetness, roundness, and so on. Occurrences of wetness or of feelings of pain, on the other hand, look like they might pass the test. What are the different parts of a pain that it can be broken down into? If you say that pain can be throbbing, or dull, or sharp, these are ways in which one pain can be compared to others, but this does not make a particular pain's being what it is (being painful) depend on those other things. You might think that there can't be pain without there being someone whose pain it is. But any Buddhist will say the idea behind this objection—that a self is the owner of states like pleasure and pain—has already been refuted. A Vaibhāṣika will take a more nuanced approach. They will agree that an occurrence of pain is usually (if not always) accompanied by a consciousness that is aware of that pain. Pains are usually experienced. But, they will say, to be aware is one thing and to be painful is another. These are two equally simple natures. That they usually occur together means that we will naturally associate the one with the other; we will think we can't make sense of a pain that is not felt. But is the nature of pain itself a composite of two components, hurting and being aware? The Vaibhāṣika will claim that when we reach something like pain or like consciousness, we have gotten to the basic level of unanalyzable simples, things that are as they are just in virtue of their existing.

4.2 Momentariness

We said earlier that there are three things all Buddhist philosophical schools agree on: mereological nihilism, the intrinsic nature criterion, and momentariness. We have discussed the first and will say more about the role of the second in Vaibhāṣika thought. We now come to the most shocking of the three, momentariness. We recall that the Buddha held all existing things to be impermanent. To say of something that it is impermanent is to say that it will go out of existence at some time or other, sooner or later. The doctrine of momentariness says that this going out of existence happens sooner rather than later—indeed, soon*est*. When something comes into existence, when it begins to exist, it immediately turns around and goes out of existence. Its existence lasts only a moment—hence the name "momentariness." Of course, this seems to fly in the face of our experience. The floor I feel beneath my feet right now seems to have lasted for more than just an instant, since otherwise, wouldn't I have fallen into the room below? The answer is that while the atoms that made up the floor a moment ago no longer exist, other atoms came into existence to take their place, and it is those atoms that are preventing me from falling right now. Likewise, when these cease to exist, there will be others to hold me up—unless, that is, a bomb goes off. The idea here is that the presently existing atoms typically cause new replacement atoms in the next moment, as long as things remain the same in the vicinity.

Why, though, don't we ever see this going out of existence that happens each moment? The example used in response to this question is someone holding a burning torch in their arm and whirling it around in a circle. To the observer, it will look like there is a wheel of fire, but in fact, there is just the one flame at just one point at each moment. Because the flame is moving so fast, we seem to see a complete circle of fire, but this is only because the lit end of the torch is moving too fast for us to detect. The same thing holds for the points of light on a video screen. These are refreshed from one moment to the next, but in a way that makes it undetectable to us. A red dot might seem to remain on screen for a while, but this is only because the refresh rate makes the replacement of one by another happen too fast for us to see.

Now we said that this doctrine of momentariness is shocking and hard to swallow. We've just seen how a defender of the doctrine would claim it is not contradicted by the evidence of our senses. But now you could say: even if momentariness is compatible with our every-day experience, the same can be said of the view that some existing things last for longer than a moment. Is it one continuously existing set of floor atoms holding me up from one moment to the next, or is it a series of floor atoms, each replaced by a new one in the next moment? Maybe our experience would be the same in either event. But then why should I believe this outlandish theory that everything vanishes each moment? Why not retain the commonsense view that most things stick around at least for a while?

As you might have come to expect by now, there is a philosophical argument that was developed to try to prove momentariness. This was not a Vaibhāṣika argument; their theory of time is a little different from the one we're about to look at (though, in the end, their view is equivalent to the momentariness view). It was devised by members of another Abhidharma school. It is called the argument from destruction since it starts from the premise that every existing thing is subject to destruction or perishing. This is what the Buddha was saying when he said that all existing things are impermanent—that sooner or later, each thing we find in the world will cease to exist. The theory of momentariness says that this ceasing will come sooner rather than later, but why? The answer comes from understanding what it means to say that something is the cause of something else. Buddhists all accept the doctrine of dependent origination, and according to that doctrine, every event or happening has a cause. The perishing of an existing thing looks like an event, so how does it happen? Is it the effect of some cause?

There are two possible ways that the perishing of an existing thing might happen. The first is that some cause brings about this event of its destruction. Suppose a glass breaks when the cat pushes it off the shelf, and it falls to the floor.[2] We might then think that the cat pushing it off the shelf caused the perishing of the glass. Now the cat pushing the glass off the shelf is something that is *extrinsic* to the existence of the glass: it isn't something that's somehow built into the nature of

---

2. What we call a glass is really a large collection of *rūpa dharma*s: many earth atoms arranged in a certain way. Strictly speaking, there is no such thing as the glass. But we'll use it as our example anyway, simply because it's easier to say "the glass" than to say "many earth atoms arranged glass-wise."

the glass itself that it would be destroyed by the cat's action. There are lots of other ways the glass might have broken. So to say that the destruction was caused is to say that it comes from outside the thing that is destroyed. Now, this sounds reasonable, but there is one other possibility: that the destruction of the glass was *intrinsic* to it, that it was the nature of the glass itself to go out of existence. It may sound odd to say that, in essence, the glass self-destructed, but we do have to agree that this is possible logically speaking. Either something else caused the perishing of the glass, or else the glass was of such a nature as to cease to exist on its own. Destruction of an existing thing must be either extrinsic (due to some distinct cause) or else intrinsic to the thing itself.

The strategy of the argument will be to prove that destruction is intrinsic by ruling out the possibility that it is extrinsic. Here is how that is done. To call something a cause is to say it produces a real effect. If something were just to sit there and never bring anything else into the world, we couldn't call it a cause. But now consider the destruction of the glass. To say the glass has been destroyed is to say that the glass is no more, that there is now the absence of that glass. So if the cat pushing the glass was the cause of its destruction, that pushing had as its effect this absence of the glass. But here's the key question: Is an absence a real thing? Consider all the things existing in the room where you are now: the floor, the walls, the ceiling, the windows, the lights, some furniture, and so on. But since it's very unlikely that there's an elephant in this room right now, we could also say that there is the absence of elephant in the room. Why don't we count this as one of the things in the room? Well, when you came into the room, did you notice the absence of elephant? Why not? Clearly, because you weren't expecting to see an elephant there. That you can now attest to the absence of elephant in the room brings out the fact that absences are dependent not just on what exists—a completely visible table, for instance—but also on what we expect. This means that absences are not ultimately, objectively real; we think of them as real only due to something subjective, our expectations. So the destruction of that glass—the occurrence of its absence—is not strictly speaking real. And since something unreal can't be a real effect, this, in turn, means that the cat pushing the glass off the shelf is not the cause of the destruction of the glass. The cat's action may have caused something (we'll see what that is in a moment), but it cannot be the cause of the absence of the glass. More generally, destruction or perishing is not extrinsic to existing things; it is not something that some outside force brings about. But there is destruction. So destruction must be intrinsic.

This does not yet show that existing things are momentary, though. There's one more step before we arrive at the conclusion of momentariness. We take that step by thinking about what it means to say that some property is intrinsic to an entity. Suppose we agreed that diamonds are intrinsically hard—that something isn't a diamond unless it is (among other things) very hard. We know that diamonds are produced when pure carbon, such as a piece of coal, is subjected to very high heat and pressure. The coal may be relatively soft, while the diamond is hard. When did the diamond first become hard? The answer must be that the diamond became hard when it came into existence. It's not as if first the diamond was produced, and then it got hard. To say that hardness is intrinsic to the diamond is to say that this property is manifested as soon as the entity comes into existence. Now apply this to the point that destruction is intrinsic to an existing thing. If destruction is intrinsic, it must be manifested as soon as the entity comes into existence. And how is destruction manifested? It is manifested in the going out of existence of the entity in question. So the instant something comes into existence, it must immediately go out of existence. If all existing things are impermanent, then all existing things must be momentary. Nothing exists for longer than a moment.

So the destruction of the glass was not caused by the cat's action. The glass went out of existence at that moment because it was its nature to cease to exist. The cat did do something, though: it caused the coming into existence of the glass shards that are now on the floor.

If the cat had not pushed the glass, then there would still be a glass on the shelf. Not the same one. The glass that the cat pushed was going to go out of existence anyway since every existing thing goes out of existence the moment immediately after the one in which it first exists. The question was just what would come into existence when that glass was destroyed. Had the cat not acted (and also no bomb had gone off in the room, etc.), then another glass just like it would have come into existence. Because of the cat's push, it is shards that exist rather than a glass. What comes into existence in the next moment depends not just on what exists now, but also on the conditions that hold now. Under normal conditions, things similar to what now exist will come into existence. This is why the world seems to exhibit so much stability. That glass seemed to have lasted from the day we bought it until just now because under normal circumstances, a glass at one moment is replaced by another one just like it in the next moment. The cat just changed the prevailing circumstances.

What we think of as a persisting object like a glass is really a series of objects, each of which exists for a moment and then goes out of existence but gives rise to a similar object in the next moment. The glass is a causal series of similarly arranged momentary *rūpa dharmas*. This is the ultimate truth. But because this is ultimately true, it is conventionally true that this glass existed from the day it was manufactured, through the day we bought it, until the day the cat broke it. That's the description of the real facts that is useful for us, given our interests and cognitive limitations. Because this description is built around accommodations to facts about us, it is not strictly speaking true. There is a gap between how things truly are and how things ordinarily seem to us. The gap doesn't seem to matter in daily life. It does matter, though, if we want our lives to be grounded in how things ultimately are. Or so say the Vaibhāṣikas. Coming to see that there really is nothing else besides momentary *dharmas*, things that bear their natures intrinsically and that come into existence in accordance with strict causal laws, is necessary if we truly want to overcome suffering.

4.3 The Soteriological Point for Vaibhāṣika

We began with three claims accepted by all schools of Buddhist philosophy: mereological nihilism, the intrinsic nature criterion, and
momentariness. We now know how schools like Vaibhāṣika understood and defended these three claims. We may still be inclined to
wonder, though, just what the point of all this is. It may be all well
and good to develop elaborate systems laying out how things truly are
behind their everyday appearance. What, though, is the point if it isn't
just to show off intellectually? (This is always a danger with scholastic
systems, and one that Buddhists were well aware of.)

There may be a clue to be found by looking at the sorts of *dharma*s
that receive the greatest attention in Vaibhāṣika theorizing. We have,
for the most part, been discussing *rūpa dharma*s like earth and water
atoms, but there are fewer kinds of these in their catalog of ultimately
real entities. There are far more different kinds of *nāma dharma*s, the
ultimately real entities that remain "after division and analysis" of
what we think of as the mind. Earlier we used a pain sensation as an
example of a *nāma dharma*, but this is just one of a very large number
of mental factors that are said to remain when we apply the intrinsic
nature test to what goes on in our mental lives. There are, for instance,
six different kinds of consciousness *dharma*s, with consciousness understood as the bare awareness of some object. There are feelings such as
pride, anger, and faith. There are unconscious mental forces such as
the associative dispositions that explain our understanding a certain
word to refer to a particular object. And so on. This attention to mental
phenomena may not seem surprising in a tradition that also empha-
sizes the practice of meditation. But it's important to bear in mind that
mereological nihilism rules out our usual way of understanding mental phenomena—as events occurring in an enduring thing, the mind.
There is ultimately no such thing as "the mind," just the many causally
interacting momentary events that we have bundled together under
that conceptual fiction. And there is a strong temptation to consider

the mind as the true "I." If the goal is to overcome the "I"-sense, then the focus on mental phenomena would make sense.

It is important that the mental *dharma*s are things whose natures are intrinsic and that they are momentary. The importance of momentariness will be obvious: if my belief in an enduring mind is just like my belief in an enduring glass, it becomes easier to dismiss the enduring "I" as a myth. It may be less obvious why it would matter that they have intrinsic natures. Think, though, about how we describe what happens when we feel a pain. We might say, "I feel it, it hurts, I don't like it, I want to make it stop." We already know that the "it hurts" part is accounted for by the occurrence of a pain *dharma*. The "feel" part, we would suppose, reflects the occurrence of a consciousness *dharma*. The disliking and the desiring represent two more kinds of *dharma*s. Now not only is it true that there is no puppet-master behind the scenes choreographing this succession of states, it is also true that each of these occurrences is what it is independently of the others in the dance of the successive mental states. That the steps in the sequence proceed as they do is nothing more than a matter of the causal laws being as they are. It is not built into the nature of a pain *dharma* that it will lead to aversion. With different causal laws, that very feeling might be succeeded by desire instead. When applied to the ultimate constituents of the mind, the intrinsic nature criterion dissipates the sense of agency we usually have with respect to our mental lives. And that sense of agency is an important component in our belief in a self. Our "I"-sense is importantly tied to the idea of a subject of our thoughts and feelings, an initiator of our actions—the one who does the thinking and feeling and makes the decisions. If we can dissolve that sense into many different components, we might be on the way to overcoming the sense of an enduring "I."

Some Key Points of Sections 4.1–4.3

- The argument for mereological nihilism is built around the idea that a whole could be neither identical with the parts (it is one while they are many) nor distinct from the parts (the place where the whole would go is already occupied by the parts).

• An ultimately real entity (a *dharma*) must be something whose nature is independent of how other things are in the world.

• The argument for momentariness turns on the point that absences are not objectively real things, so when something goes out of existence, it makes no sense to say that its destruction (its absence) is the real effect of some real cause.

4.4 Yogācāra and Madhyamaka As Mahāyāna Schools

At around the beginning of the Common Era, a new tendency arose in Indian Buddhist thought, the Mahāyāna movement. This did not start out as a development in philosophy. As far as we can now tell, it first appeared in the form of sūtras that purported to reveal teachings of the Buddha and other enlightened beings that were not disclosed in earlier collections of his discourses (the *Nikāyas*). There is little by way of philosophical analysis or argumentation in these early Mahāyāna sūtras. They put forward, largely without argument, two new ideas that became central to Mahāyāna: the bodhisattva ideal and the doctrine of emptiness. A bodhisattva is someone who overcomes ignorance about the self but refrains from entering final nirvāna, instead choosing to be reborn in order to help others overcome suffering. Mahāyāna claims that it is better to be a bodhisattva than to be an *arhat*, the ideal figure according to schools like Vaibhāṣika. The doctrine of emptiness holds that all things are empty (*śūnya*) of essence. Now the earlier schools teach that persons are devoid of essence insofar as they lack a self. But Mahāyāna claims that this does not go far enough. The ultimate truth, it claims, is that all *dharma*s also lack essence, insofar as they are devoid of intrinsic nature. It is only several centuries later, though, that we see the beginnings of two philosophical schools that develop and try to support these new doctrines. These are the schools known as Yogācāra and Madhyamaka.

We won't discuss the disagreement between Mahāyāna and Abhidharma over the bodhisattva ideal. What does require discussion is the teaching of universal emptiness. It was said earlier that all of the major schools accept three things, one of them being that ultimately real things must have intrinsic nature. If, as Mahāyāna claims, nothing has intrinsic nature, wouldn't that mean that nothing whatsoever exists? And isn't that obviously absurd? It's one thing to say that chariots, trees, houses, and even persons don't exist (since they depend on their parts). But it's a far different thing to say that even the parts making up those things are unreal. In fact, the two Mahāyāna schools of Yogācāra and Madhyamaka do agree that if there were ultimately real things, then they would have intrinsic natures. So in that sense, they do accept the doctrine of intrinsic natures. Yogācāra tries to escape the absurdity of metaphysical nihilism[3]—the claim that absolutely nothing exists—by interpreting the doctrine of emptiness as saying that we are wrong about the sorts of things that can be the intrinsic natures of ultimately real things. It takes its job to be showing what that mistake is and how to correct it. It is Madhyamaka that takes the doctrine of emptiness literally and thus denies that there is anything that is ultimately real. But we'll come back to that later, and start with Yogācāra.

4.5 Yogācāra Idealism

This school is also known as the "Consciousness-Only" school. As the name suggests, it denies an external physical world; there are, it

---

3. A nihilist is someone who believes that something commonly thought of as real does not actually exist. An ethical nihilist, for instance, is someone who holds that ethical values do not exist. Metaphysical nihilism is the view that absolutely nothing exists. This is different from mereological nihilism, which is the view that composite or partite entities don't exist. A mereological nihilist would turn into a metaphysical nihilist if they added that non-composite objects also don't exist.

maintains, only states of consciousness or awareness. Yogācāra philosophers are not the only ones to deny the existence of anything physical, anything existing outside the mind. The eighteenth-century British philosopher George Berkeley said something similar. Berkeley's view is called "subjective idealism." It says that there are only minds and the ideas or mental states that occur in them; there are no physical objects (including the body and the brain). Yogācāra is also an idealism, but it claims that there is no mind or subject in which mental states occur, there are only the mental states themselves, so it would be better to call it "subject-less idealism."[4]

The first response to an idealist is usually to say that our sensory experience is constantly informing us about the physical world around us. Isn't it obvious that there are tables and chairs, rocks and trees, since we can see and feel them? The Yogācāra response is that we also have the experience of "seeing" things in dreams or seeing a second moon when we are drunk or dizzy. No one thinks that the monster seen in a dream really exists, so why think that the things seen in waking experience do? A realist about the external world (for short, a realist) will object that dreams and illusory waking experiences don't fit in with ordinary waking experiences; they also lack the feature of being had by other observers (of being publicly verifiable). The Yogācāra idealist replies that ordinary waking experiences are caused not by interaction with physical objects but by the ripening of karmic seeds in accordance with the karmic causal laws. It's because we formed certain intentions in the past that present circumstances have generated certain mental states, ones that we misinterpret as coming from outside. That our experiences generally agree with those of others is explained by the fact that we share similar karma.

---

4. We'll just call it idealism. It should be pointed out, though, that some modern scholars deny that Yogācāra taught idealism. We won't be discussing their interpretation. The interpretation presented here is how other classical Indian philosophers understood Yogācāra.

The "ripening of karmic seeds" account of our waking sensory experience will sound odd to those who don't believe in karma and rebirth. Yogācāra idealists engage in a long debate with their realist opponents over this account, but we won't go into that here. Even if the idealist won that debate, there is still the problem that all they will have given us is an alternative scenario concerning how our sensory experiences are caused. Showing that this alternative scenario could be true is not the same as showing that it is true and the realist account is false. At best, it would only show that realism could, *for all we know*, be false. It might turn us into skeptics about the existence of the external world, but that's not the same thing as becoming idealists. Yogācāra needs stronger arguments. One place they find them is in the fact that physical things are infinitely divisible: everything physical, no matter how small, can always be cut in half.

Remember that ultimately real things or *dharma*s are things that retain their nature "after division and analysis." A realist might suppose that things like a pot exist, but when we separate the top and bottom halves, there is no longer a pot. There are still the bits of fired clay, but those can be analyzed into occurrences of hardness, of red color, and so on. So let's take an occurrence of hardness: How big is it? If it has some size, then it can be divided. If, on the other hand, it has no size, how will we ever be able to feel it? To say that it is an occurrence of hardness is to say that when something else comes in contact with it, it resists, stopping that other thing from moving to its other side and then beyond. But this means that resistance (the intrinsic nature of this supposed *dharma*) requires that the occurrence of hardness have two different sides. And something that is a mere point, that does not have any size, does not have two different sides. No matter how many point-size occurrences of hardness we pack together, we'll never get anything big enough to detect through the sense of touch. Its size is zero, and $0 + 0 + \ldots + 0 = 0$. If an occurrence of hardness has some size, then it is not ultimately real because it is divisible; if it has no size, then it could not explain our experience of touching. And the same considerations apply to the other kinds of sensory experience as well. So the realist cannot explain how external objects bring about our experience. The Yogācāra karmic seeds account does not have this problem. Their conclusion is that they win the debate.

This is not the only argument Yogācāra philosophers developed to support their idealism. It does, though, give a good feel for how they approach the job. We won't try to evaluate the argument; all we can do here is examine how it might fit into the basic Buddhist project of overcoming suffering. What could possibly be the point, for a Buddhist, of denying the existence of the physical world? It might be thought that this would be a good way of overcoming materialistic desires. If there really are no physical objects, then it wouldn't make sense to hanker after shiny baubles or the latest technological marvel. What this overlooks, though, is that idealists don't deny that we have the experience of wearing the shiny bauble or using the cool device. We can still hanker after the experience, even if we're wrong to think the experience is caused by a physical object. So this would not be a good reason for a Buddhist to embrace idealism.

The point of Buddhist idealism is more subtle. Common sense distinguishes between two different realms, the objective and the subjective, the world "out there" and the world "in here." The first is supposed to be public, available to all, while the second is thought of as private, known only to the subject whose inner life it is. Yogācāra's idealism is the denial that there actually is such a thing as an objective external world. Suppose they can prove that this is true. Now notice that "inner" and "outer" are contrast terms. Just as there can't be left without right, north without south, so if there is no outer realm of physical objects, it may not make sense to call experience something inner or subjective. But if we can no longer think of experiences as subjective, we can't think of them as belonging to a subject that has them as its experiences. Idealism might, in other words, be an interesting way to make the basic Buddhist point of non-self.

Nowadays, many people think that there really is nothing more to reality than the physical things that science tells us about. They suspect that what we commonly think of as the mind is really just the brain and that our thoughts and experiences are just brain events, the firing of neurons. Some people who believe this but are also interested in Buddhism think that this might be a good way to show that the Buddhists are right about non-self. If nothing in the brain could have all the properties that the self would have, this would show that there is no self. No Indian Buddhists accepted physicalism (the view that only physical things are real). Vaibhāṣikas, for instance, held that there are both physical and mental *dharma*s. What is interesting about Yogācāra idealism is that it might also turn out to be a way to show there is no self. It isn't only physicalism that can be used to support the Buddhist teaching of non-self; idealism can as well.

4.6 Yogācāra and Intrinsic Natures

We said earlier that all three of the schools we are looking at accept, in one way or another, mereological nihilism, the intrinsic nature criterion, and momentariness. That Yogācāra accepts mereological nihilism will be clear from the use they make of it in their infinite divisibility argument against realism. We haven't touched on momentariness, but Yogācāra holds that as well. What, though, of the claim that the ultimate reals must have intrinsic nature? Since Yogācāra is a Mahāyāna school, must it not reject that claim to square its theory with the Mahāyāna doctrine that all *dharma*s are devoid of intrinsic nature?

Yogācāra authors are well aware that given their other commitments, a literal understanding of the Mahāyāna doctrine could lead them to metaphysical nihilism, so they try very hard to develop a different understanding of the Mahāyāna teaching of emptiness. This effort starts with the point that someone who believes that there are physical objects will think that their being physical or existing outside the mind is intrinsic to those objects. Vaibhāṣikas would certainly say that being external is intrinsic to the *rūpa dharmas*. They would say that an occurrence of wetness is not only something that would have the nature of being wet regardless of whether or not anything else existed but would likewise be what it is regardless of whether or not it was perceived. (Physical things are precisely the things we think of as continuing to exist when no one perceives them.) But if idealism is true, nothing can exist unperceived. So this particular candidate for the status of being an intrinsic nature would turn out to be something we wrongly superimposed on the world, something that *dharmas* are empty of.

Now there is a second step we can take. If the point raised earlier about "objective" and "subjective" being contrast terms is right, we can say that *dharmas* are equally devoid of the nature of being mental or conscious states. And that is likewise a nature that we are ordinarily inclined to superimpose on some of the things we think exist. If nothing that is ultimately real can be said to be "outside," it cannot make sense to say that things are "inside" either. Inside of what? While we may still say that there are things that exist ultimately, we may not call them either external or internal. Yogācāra's idealism has the interesting consequence that reality is non-dual in nature: devoid of the duality of subject and object, of consciousness and the things that consciousness is aware of. And this should make us wonder: If the ultimately real things cannot be described in either way, what can be said about them? And the Yogācāra answer is: nothing. To attribute a certain nature to something, to say what it is like, is to look for ways in which it resembles certain other things. And that requires that we think of it and those other things as possible objects of experience. If nothing can ultimately be an object of experience, then it seems we cannot say of anything ultimately real that it has a certain intrinsic nature. All that we can say about such a thing is that it is what it is, that it is distinct from everything else. And to say that is to say nothing at all. The ultimately real is beyond language and inexpressible.

This may make you wonder how it's possible, according to Yogācāra, to become enlightened. If the cessation of suffering requires that one come to know how things truly are, but how things truly are is ineffable, how could one ever directly grasp this? The answer to this question may lie in the school's name, "Yogācāra," which literally means "the practice of yoga." The practice of meditation is important in all schools of Buddhist philosophy, but the name of this school tells us it was especially important to the founders of Yogācāra. In certain key Yogācāra texts, it is claimed that becoming enlightened involves attaining a state of non-dual awareness that is devoid of all conceptualization, just a pure seeing without any sense of a distinction between the seeing and what is seen. This state is said to come after mastery of a series of increasingly rarefied meditative states, and its attainment is said to bring home in a visceral way what has already been conveyed through the arguments for idealism: that reality is ultimately non-dual and so is inexpressible in nature.

Yogācāra does accept the view that only things with intrinsic nature can ultimately be real. And it holds that there are ultimately real things. It reconciles this with the key Mahāyāna claim that all things (including the things that are thought to be ultimately real) are empty of intrinsic nature by reinterpreting "intrinsic nature" to mean something that requires the subject-object dichotomy. We go wrong, it claims, when we try to say what the ultimately real is like, when we try to express its nature. When we do that, we are presupposing a distinction between the things to be grasped and the grasping of those things. Reality itself is devoid of that distinction, they claim, but there is such a thing as ultimate reality. Metaphysical nihilism is thereby avoided.

Some Key Points of Sections 4.5–4.6

- The Yogācāra teaching of consciousness-only is the denial of the existence of a physical world; our sensory experience is caused by the ripening of karmic seeds in a mental continuum.

- One important argument for consciousness-only turns on the problem of explaining how anything without parts can have any size.

- The soteriological point of consciousness-only is to undermine the idea of a self by dissolving the contrast between what's "in here" and what's "out there."

4.7 Madhyamaka and Intrinsic Natures

Unlike the other two schools we have discussed so far, the Madhyamaka school has a single founder, Nāgārjuna (second century CE). His work was the first attempt we know of to make systematic philosophical sense of the Mahāyāna doctrine of emptiness. Where Yogācāra tries to dodge the bullet of metaphysical nihilism by reinterpreting that doctrine, Nāgārjuna embraces a literal understanding of the doctrine. He and later Mādhyamikas (members of the Madhyamaka school) insist that they are not metaphysical nihilists. But how exactly they think they can avoid that (absurd) result is a matter of some dispute among modern scholars. Here we'll be describing one way of interpreting early Madhyamaka, but you should know that there are other ways of reading it as well. Indeed Madhyamaka's rivals among classical Indian philosophers, Buddhist and non-Buddhist alike, didn't know exactly what to make of it. So it's no wonder that the reading we are about to embark on should be controversial.

One thing to be made clear at the outset is that Madhyamaka accepts both mereological nihilism and the intrinsic nature criterion for ultimate reals. The argument for mereological nihilism that we looked at earlier discusses two different ways in which there might be real wholes in addition to real parts—the whole might be identical with its parts or distinct from its parts. The Mādhyamika author Candrakīrti developed an argument that looks at three additional ways in which whole and parts might be related and argues that none of the five will work. Wholes cannot be ultimately real; the composite things that we think of as existing are really just conceptual fictions. And from this it follows that an ultimately real entity must have its nature intrinsically; its nature cannot be something it borrows from other things in the way that the chariot borrows its shape from the shapes of its parts. To say this, though, is just to say that *if* there are things that are ultimately real, *then* they must have intrinsic natures. It leaves open the possibility that there may be no such things as ultimately real *dharmas*.

Madhyamaka texts are full of arguments, but these arguments are of a distinctive sort. We expect an argument to try to prove its conclusion, but Madhyamaka arguments aim at something else. They start from an assumption that an opponent holds and then try to demonstrate that this assumption, together with other views the opponent accepts, leads to a result the opponent must reject, such as a contradiction. This style of argument resembles what is called a *reductio ad absurdum* (Latin for "reduction to absurdity"), but a *reductio* argument usually contains a positive conclusion, namely that the hypothesis being examined is false. All that Madhyamaka arguments try to show is that the opponent should not hold the view in question; they don't try to prove that that view is false and some other view is true. This fact about their strategy holds an important clue to what Mādhyamikas are up to. When they argue that the views of their opponents about the ultimately real entities are problematic, they are not trying to prove some other view about what ultimate reality is like. They are trying to help their opponents stop constructing theories about ultimate reality.

4.8 Some Madhyamaka Arguments against Intrinsic Natures

To see how this strategy works, we should look (briefly) at some examples of Madhyamaka arguments. One such argument concerns the claim that ultimately real things undergo origination and destruction, that they come into and go out of existence. When we discussed the doctrine of momentariness (§2), you may have found yourself wondering how something completely simple like a *dharma* could undergo cessation immediately after it came into existence. Does this cessation happen at the same time as its origination happens? If you thought this was odd, Mādhyamika would agree. Origination and cessation, i.e., creation and destruction, are opposite actions. For something to originate is for it to begin to exist. For something to be destroyed is for it to stop existing. How can both things happen at once? The argument for momentariness was supposed to show that when something comes into existence, it goes out of existence right afterward. The fact that origination and cessation can't be simultaneous would suggest that the *dharma* sticks around for a moment before it manifests its intrinsic cessation by going out of existence. This was close to the view of some Abhidharma schools, which held that *dharma*s go through three phases: origination, maintenance, and cessation. But that seems to require that the *dharma* lasts for three instants, not just one, which contradicts momentariness. So it looks like if we are going to follow this three-phase idea, we have to say that the *dharma* only exists during the middle moment of maintenance; the moment of origination must be before it exists, the moment of cessation being after it has ceased. Will this work?

The Mādhyamika suggests it won't by raising a difficult question: Is there really such a thing as the present moment? Isn't the present really just the dividing point between the past and the future? And since a point has no extension, it doesn't seem to make sense to say that something exists *in* the present. The idea of saying that a *dharma* exists during the moment of maintenance was that then there would be an interval between the moment of origination and the moment of cessation. But if the present isn't actually a moment, just the point where the past ends and the future begins, we seem back where we started, saying that origination and cessation both happen at the same time. The idea that there are simple things, *dharma*s, that are momentary seems to be in trouble.

To say this is not, though, to suggest that the ultimately real things could be non-momentary either. If *dharmas* were not momentary, then they might be things that endure for some time between when they come into existence and when they perish, or else they might be eternal. But something that is both simple (like a *dharma*) and eternal could not make any difference to the world since it couldn't cause anything to happen. In order for something to act as a cause, it must undergo a change, and the only change a simple thing can undergo is its perishing, something an eternal thing can never do. But causation is likewise ruled out for a *dharma* that was impermanent but lasted more than a moment. Since a *dharma* is something with just one nature, its intrinsic nature, the only way it can change is for it to lose that nature. And to lose that nature is to go out of existence. So a *dharma* couldn't act as a cause and then continue to exist for a while before it went out of existence. It follows that a *dharma* couldn't be non-momentary and still make some difference to the way the world is. But in order for something to exist, surely it must have some impact on the rest of reality. So the thesis that there are non-momentary *dharmas* seems to run into difficulties too.

Notice that the Mādhyamika is not arguing that *dharmas* must be some way other than momentary or non-momentary (such as that they are ineffable). They aren't saying anything positive about *dharmas* at all. They are just pointing out difficulties in a particular theory about what the ultimately real *dharmas* might be like. Another Madhyamaka argument is aimed at a view that both Vaibhāṣika and Yogācāra hold—that *dharmas* are the causes of the arising of other *dharmas*. We have already seen how both schools use this idea to explain why we (in their view wrongly) believe there are enduring physical objects and enduring minds: one momentary *dharma* can cause a similar *dharma* to come into existence in the next moment so that it feels like there is one enduring thing. But how does causation actually work at the ultimate level? The stock example of causation for Indian philosophers is when a seed brings a sprout into existence.[5] Many people would agree to call the seed the cause of the sprout, but we know that conditions have to be right for the seed to bring a sprout into existence: the seed must be planted in warm moist soil, and so on. So is it the aggregate of seed, soil, moisture, and so on that should be called the cause, the thing that actually produces the sprout? The problem with saying this is that an aggregate is clearly a whole made of parts and so is not itself really real. And something that is unreal can't be the cause of anything. So the sensible thing to say, it seems, is that the seed comes to be the cause of the sprout in the presence of the conditions of being in warm moist soil. Those conditions endow the seed with a causal power that it exercises by producing a sprout.

Suppose this is right. We will now want to know just how this producing works. To say that the seed produces the sprout is to say that it is what endows its effect, the sprout, with the specific nature of the sprout. We don't expect a seed to produce a toaster oven, and when it's a rice seed we're talking about, we expect its product to be a rice sprout and not a barley sprout. Is this because the seed already contains within itself the nature of a sprout? While this thesis might be tempting, it doesn't make sense when we think about it. If the sprout already existed in the seed, why didn't the seed look and behave like a sprout? If the nature of the effect is already found in the cause, then the effect is not something that is produced. To be produced is to come into existence from the state of not yet existing. So the sprout must be distinct from the seed, something with a new nature that was not there when all we had was the seed.

We've now narrowed down our options to just one: the seed comes to have the power to produce a sprout through the conditions (warm, moist soil, etc.), and it exercises this power by producing a new thing

---

5. Of course, neither a seed nor a sprout can be a *dharma*. Both are wholes made of parts. These are used as examples simply to illustrate the different possibilities concerning how the causal relation might work.

with a new nature, a sprout. When, though, does this producing occur, before the sprout arises, or after it has arisen? We can think of this producing as a matter of the cause conferring on the effect the nature that makes the effect be the sort of thing it is—in our example, the nature of being a rice sprout. But the conferring relation seems to require the existence of both parties to the relation, both the thing doing the conferring and the thing that receives what is conferred. And now we run into an obstacle: cause must precede effect so that when the cause exists the effect does not exist, and when the effect does exist, the cause no longer does. Producing means conferring, and conferring requires simultaneous existence, but cause and effect never exist simultaneously. You might think that conferring doesn't necessarily require that both the conferrer and the conferee exist at the same time. When a will is executed, for instance, something is conferred on a beneficiary after the maker of the will is deceased. But that conferring is actually done by the executor of the will, who does exist at the same time as the beneficiary. This might make you wonder what was wrong with the idea that the seed confers the nature of a sprout on its effect when both exist. But if the sprout already exists, there should be no need to produce it. Production can't happen when the effect already exists. And when the effect does not yet exist, the seed can't do its work of producing.

It looks, then, like there may be some difficulties in the idea of causation that other Buddhist philosophers used in their accounts of the nature of ultimate reality. Does this mean there really are no causal connections between things that happen in the world, and things just happen at random, for no reason at all? Some people might draw that conclusion, but Mādhyamikas would ask them why, in that case, you can't get a toaster oven from a rice seed. We do observe regularities in the world, and someone who says there really are no causal relations will have a tough time explaining that. Here it's important to notice that the problems we've been discussing have to do with how ultimately real *dharma*s could stand in cause-effect relations. We don't run into these problems when we consider the production of conventionally real things like chariots or pots. The production of a pot is a gradual process: first, the clay is thrown on the wheel, shaped and dried, then it is fired, then it is glazed and fired again. We might say that during this process, the pot is undergoing production. When we say this, we seem to be thinking of the pot as something that goes through a process of coming into existence, a process that takes some time. So it might make sense to say that the cause of the pot confers the nature of a pot on the effect at a time when both exist. We can say this, though, because a pot is a whole made of parts. Its coming into existence involves the arranging of those parts, something that can take some time. Not so with a *dharma*, the existence of which has to be all-or-nothing. Either a given *dharma* is there, or else it's not; there is no in-between. This means, though, that we may still be able to make sense of the idea of causation as a relation between things that are conventionally real. If the Madhyamaka argument shows anything, it's just that the theories of causation propounded by other Buddhist philosophers to explain how things ultimately are might not work.

There are many other Madhyamaka arguments against theories about things with intrinsic nature. But this is not the place to investigate them. Instead, we should summarize how things stand at this point. Madhyamaka accepts the claim that wholes are not ultimately real, that only things with intrinsic nature could be ultimately real, and that ultimate reals would have to be momentary. They also give arguments that they think show that things with intrinsic nature could not participate in causal relations and could not presently exist. Suppose the arguments really do show what they claim. Suppose, too, that there is no other theory that could get around the problems Madhyamaka indicates. Where would that leave us? Clearly, this would mean that there can be no ultimately real things, no *dharma*s. And isn't that equivalent to metaphysical nihilism, the absurd view that the other Mahāyāna school, Yogācāra, tried so hard to avoid? Well, but the metaphysical nihilist tells us what they think ultimate reality is like—that nothing exists. A Buddhist metaphysical nihilist would put that as: only things with intrinsic natures could be ultimately real, and all the supposedly ultimately real things are empty or devoid of intrinsic nature, so the ultimate nature of reality is that nothing exists. Here is another way to put that: emptiness is the intrinsic nature of the ultimately real things. But now, here is something else that Madhyamaka says: emptiness is itself empty. That is, emptiness is not the intrinsic nature of anything ultimately real. This makes sense if you think about it. A property can be the nature of some entity only if that entity exists. If there are no entities that are ultimately real, then it would be a mistake to say that they bear the property of being empty. This suggests a way that Mādhyamikas might avoid the absurd result of nihilism. They might say that the very idea of how things ultimately are simply makes no sense. They might say that we should abandon the project of doing metaphysics, of looking for the ultimate nature of reality. Not because the project is too hard for us, but because it is incoherent. To use a stock Indian example, looking for the ultimate nature of reality is like searching for the son or daughter of a barren woman.

4.9 The Soteriological Point of Madhyamaka Emptiness

While Yogācāra interprets the Mahāyāna thesis of emptiness as the claim that reality is non-dual and ineffable, Madhyamaka (according to this interpretation) takes it to be saying that the very idea of the ultimate nature of reality is incoherent. In place of the metaphysical realism of Yogācāra (and of Vaibhāṣika), Madhyamaka recommends metaphysical quietism, the abandonment of the search for the correct theory about how things really, truly are. How might that fit into the Buddhist project of seeking the cessation of suffering? Some take it to mean that we should simply stop thinking so hard about what the world is like and take it to be what common sense says it is: a world of enduring objects, including enduring persons with minds and bodies. This might sound appealing; doing metaphysics is hard work. But it doesn't seem to fit well with the project that all Buddhists take as definitive of their tradition: overcoming suffering by dispelling the illusion of an "I" and the attitudes based on it. It isn't clear how a Buddhist can make sense of the central teaching of non-self without doing some metaphysics, that is, digging beneath the surface of our conventional reality to find something more objective. In fact, Mādhyamikas agree that we should follow the path laid out in Early Buddhism and Abhidharma, a path of using reason to reveal the cognitive errors behind our belief in a real "I." That would seem to mean doing metaphysics. So how could metaphysical quietism fit into a Buddhist project?

Here is one possible answer. Perhaps Mādhyamikas think that the paths worked out by other Buddhist schools are right for those starting out on the arduous journey to nirvāna. The thought might be that the best way to see through the illusion of the "I"-sense is to come to understand that there really can be nothing more to the enduring person than a causal series of assemblages of impermanent *dharma*s. Achieving this insight will involve doing metaphysics: mastering the argument for mereological nihilism, understanding why ultimately real things would have to have their natures intrinsically, working through the argument for momentariness, grasping the distinction between things that are ultimately real and things that are mere conceptual fictions, and so on. This work can lead to understanding not only that there is no self, but also why belief in a self is nevertheless so persuasive. And that understanding, when combined with the new habits acquired through the practice of meditation, can substantially weaken the hold of the "I"-sense. There may be one remaining obstacle, though: the idea that there is such a thing as the way that the world really, truly, objectively is, the idea of the ultimate truth. This idea can instill a kind of attachment too. (Think about how worked up people sometimes get when they debate philosophical issues.) So while it may be necessary to start out searching for the truth about how things ultimately are, at a certain point, this can turn into a hindrance. This might be the point at which the Madhyamaka understanding of emptiness comes into play. If the Madhyamaka arguments are right, we can take them to show that the idea of there being an ultimate truth was just a useful fiction, something that helped along the way to nirvāna but couldn't take us to the final destination.

Notice that if this is the idea behind the Madhyamaka strategy, it doesn't rule out the importance of philosophy in achieving the Buddhist goal of cessation of suffering. For not only would it mean that one must begin by mastering a system like Vaibhāṣika or Yogācāra, but also after doing so there would still remain some hard philosophical work: thinking through the Madhyamaka arguments meant to undermine the notion of the ultimate truth by calling into question the idea of things with intrinsic natures. It may be easy to thumb one's nose at serious metaphysics, to simply reject the project of trying to work out how things ultimately are. But people who take that stance usually do so because they're convinced that the world is a much simpler place than philosophers seem to think. And to take this stance is to hold that there is a way that things truly are, namely how common sense says things are. To think this is to hold on to the idea of how things really are. Mādhyamikas are asking us to do something really hard: give up on this idea and recognize that reality has no bedrock level, that it's useful fictions all the way down. Achieving this insight requires disciplined philosophical practice. The practice is different from what we saw with Vaibhāṣika and Yogācāra. They had us working through arguments meant to show that the world is a certain way. Madhyamaka strategy has us working through arguments meant to show that the world can't be this way, or that way, or yet another way. But they are arguments all the same. And they must be worked through. As we saw in the Introduction, Buddhist philosophers think it's not enough just to accept their conclusions on faith.

Some Key Points of Sections 4.7–4.9

- The core claim of the Madhyamaka school is that all *dharmas* are devoid of intrinsic nature; given what *dharmas* must be like, this means there are none.

- Madhyamaka can avoid the absurdity of metaphysical nihilism—the claim that nothing whatsoever exists—if its real aim is to show that the very idea of how things ultimately are makes no sense (if it is a kind of metaphysical quietism).

- Arguments for emptiness try to show that absurd consequences follow if we assume that there are ultimately real things with intrinsic natures, e.g., that nothing could ever come into existence in dependence on prior causes.

- The soteriological point of emptiness may be to induce metaphysical quietism in Buddhist practitioners, thereby ridding them of the habit of metaphysical table pounding picked up along the path.

4.10 The Rest of the Rest of the Story

The three schools of Buddhist philosophy we've looked at in this chapter were all under way in India by the fourth century CE. Buddhist thought continued to flourish in India for another eight centuries, declining only when Moghul raids sacked such great Buddhist universities as Nālandā and Vikramaśīla. Long before then, Buddhism had spread through Southeast Asia, Tibet, Mongolia, and East Asia (first to China, then to Korea and Japan). Although Buddhism did largely die out in India after the twelfth century, it has continued to flourish elsewhere in Asia up to the present day. And beginning in the nineteenth century it has found converts in the West as well. Obviously, not everyone who identifies as Buddhist is a philosopher. But the continued existence of Buddhism over the millennia has meant the continued development of Buddhist philosophy alongside other evolving practices.

In this chapter, we have discussed three quite different philo-sophical positions: Vaibhāṣika reductionism, Yogācāra idealism, and Madhyamaka metaphysical quietism. All three represent philosophi-cal elaborations of the teachings of the Buddha. But these three just scratch the surface; over time and across different regions, a variety of different philosophical systems emerge, each representing itself as an important component of Buddhist practice. You might wonder how there can be such diversity in a single soteriological tradition. But we find something similar in such religions as Christianity, Islam, and Judaism. Moreover, in the Buddhist case, there is the device of "graded teaching" to help smooth the way. A follower of Yogācāra, for instance, can use this to avoid dismissing Vaibhāṣika realism about the external world as Buddhist heresy. Instead, they can say that the Vaibhāṣika stance represents a preliminary approach for practitioners who are not yet ready for the full truth about reality, that all is consciousness-only.

It is this sort of inclusivist stance that leads to the development of a school of Indian Buddhist philosophy that completely avoids taking a stand on the issue of the reality of the external world. Two of the giants of later Indian Buddhist philosophy, Dignāga and Dharmakīrti, are known for their groundbreaking work in epistemology. The tools they created and refined help philosophers of all metaphysical persuasions work out whether their claims have adequate rational support. But we have already seen an instance of this inclusivism in the last chapter, in Śāntideva's moral obligation argument. Śāntideva was a Mādhyam-ika, someone who denies that there are things with intrinsic natures. Yet his argument turns on the point that occurrences of suffering have the intrinsic nature of to-be-prevented-ness. How can a Mādhyamika give an argument like this? By presenting it as a useful component of a path that he claims will eventually lead to full insight into the emp-tiness of all *dharmas*.

As Buddhism has become a global phenomenon, so has the study of Buddhist philosophy. There are now scholars on six continents inves-tigating the growth and development of the Buddhist philosophical tradition in Asia. Much of their scholarship aims at clarifying different parts of the tradition and making it accessible to a wider audience. But some of it can be seen as continuing that tradition. Philosophy thrives in the examination of competing views. Buddhist philosophy is no exception. As the work of the great Buddhist philosophers of the past becomes more widely available, it becomes possible to develop a dialog between Buddhist and Western philosophical traditions. Through such dialog, we can expect new and more refined Buddhist philosophy to emerge. We saw an example of this in the discussion of the "free will" problem and Buddhist ethics (Chapter 3, §5). The Buddhist philosophical tradition may be more than just an interesting historical artifact.

For Further Reading

For a thorough and sophisticated treatment of the philosophical components of the Indian Buddhist tradition see Jan Westerhoff, *The Golden Age of Indian Buddhist Philosophy* (Oxford: Oxford University Press, 2017). The development of the Indian Buddhist philosophical tradition is also discussed in some detail in my *Buddhism As Philosophy*, 2nd ed. (Indianapolis, IN: Hackett Publishing, 2021). The Introduction and first three chapters of that work largely overlap those here, but the remaining six chapters systematically examine key parts of the major schools of the later tradition.

For an overview of the history of Buddhist philosophy in Tibet, see Matthew Kapstein, "Buddhist Thought in Tibet: An Historical Introduction," in *The Oxford Handbook of World Philosophy*, ed. Jay Garfield and William Edelglass (New York: Oxford University Press, 2011), pp. 245–63.

For an account of the early history of Buddhism's entry into Tibet, including a crucial debate between representatives of Indian and Chinese Buddhist thought, see David Seyfort Ruegg, *Buddha-nature, Mind and the Problem of Gradualism in a Comparative Perspective* (London: School of Oriental and African Studies, 1989). For a fascinating account of Tibetan Buddhist monastic education, see Georges Dreyfus, *The Sound of Two Hands Clapping* (Berkeley: University of California Press, 2003).

For an excellent study of the transmission of Buddhism from India to China, see Erik Zürcher, *The Buddhist Conquest of China* (Leiden: E.J. Brill, 1972). For a discussion of Chinese Buddhist philosophy that places it within the larger Chinese philosophical tradition, see JeeLoo Liu, *An Introduction to Chinese Philosophy: From Ancient Philosophy to Chinese Buddhism* (London: Blackwell Publishing, 2006).

Glossary

annihilationism: the view that a person ceases to exist when all or some of its constituents cease to exist, even if those constituents are replaced by new ones; typically, the view that death is the end of a person's existence

convenient designator: a word that was introduced to designate many distinct things under a single label because it is more convenient to treat them as a single thing, e.g., "six-pack," "dozen," "city"

dharma: in Buddhist metaphysics, the term for an ultimately real entity

eternalism: the view that persons never cease to exist, typically held by those who believe that the essence of a person is their eternal self

inner sense (*manas*): the faculty by means of which one becomes aware of inner or mental states

intrinsic nature (*svabhāva*): a nature that is intrinsic to an entity, i.e., that it has independently of how other things are, a nature that is not borrowed from other things

lightness: the property a theory has when it posits fewer unobservable entities than rival theories in order to explain some phenomenon; also known as parsimony

means of knowledge: a procedure that invariably brings about a true cognition of a fact not previously known

mereology: that part of metaphysics concerned with the relation between wholes and their constituent parts

metaphysical realism: the view that there is such a thing as how the world is in itself, independently of the concepts that we happen to use in our thoughts about reality

nihilism (metaphysical): the view that absolutely nothing exists

numerical identity: being one and the same thing, a relation that is compatible with being qualitatively non-identical (e.g., the mango that at one time is green and at another time is yellow)

ontology: that part of metaphysics that investigates what fundamental sorts of things exist; a philosophical theory's ontology is the list of fundamental kinds of existents it acknowledges

orthodox: in classical Indian philosophy, an orthodox school is one that accepts the Vedas as authoritative texts, i.e., as conferring knowledge about super-sensible matters that can be known in no other way; Nyāya and Advaita Vedānta are orthodox schools, all Buddhist schools are heterodox

preta: a "hungry ghost," a human-like creature who, due to bad karma, is born into circumstances in which they can only eat and drink vile substances

Punctualism: the form of annihilationism that holds that persons cease to exist not at death but from any one moment to the next

qualitative identity: being alike in properties, a relation that is compatible with being numerically non-identical (e.g., two distinct mangoes that are alike in being yellow, ovoid, sweet, etc.)

quality: a property-particular, e.g., the occurrence of white color in an individual piece of paper; two property-particulars may be qualitatively identical but still numerically distinct (e.g., two pieces of paper may be exactly alike in their whiteness, yet the white color in one and the white color in the other are still two numerically distinct entities)

rūpa: the category of the physical or material; sometimes translated as "form," this being the literal meaning of the Sanskrit word, but used here to mean "that which has form or shape" (as opposed to mental entities, which lack this physical property)

skandha: the list of the five *skandhas* is one of three classifications the Buddha used to categorize all the constituents of the person; it consists of *rūpa*, the category that includes all physical things, and four kinds of mental elements: hedonic feelings, perceptual identifications, dispositions, and consciousness

śramaṇa: a wandering ascetic, someone seeking solutions to existential problems outside the prevailing ideologies

substance: a persisting entity that is the bearer of properties; most Buddhists deny that strictly speaking or ultimately there are any substances

Supplementary Source Readings

Supplementary Reading for Chapter 1

Translated from *Saṃyutta Nikāya* 1.136–41

In this passage, the Buddha discusses the connection between hankering after things that do not exist—whether external or internal to the person themselves—and suffering. The chief focus is on the "internal" side, and in particular on the non-existent self. The passage thus develops a connection between the first Nobles' truth, that there is suffering, and the second Nobles' truth, that suffering comes about due to ignorance. It may also suggest a possible answer to the question of what it is like to live without suffering.

A monk asked, "Lord, can there be anxiety about external things that do not exist?"

"There can be, O monk," said the Blessed One. "In such cases, monk, someone thinks: 'Oh, I had it! Woe is me, I no longer have it! Oh, might I have it again! But alas, I do not obtain it!' Hence he grieves, is depressed, and laments; beating his breast, he weeps and falls into bewilderment. Thus, monk, is there anxiety about external things that do not exist."

"But, Lord, can there be lack of anxiety about external things that do not exist?"

"There can be, O monk," said the Blessed One. "In such cases, monk, someone does not think: 'Oh, I had it! Woe is me, I no longer have it! Oh, might I have it again! But alas, I do not obtain it!' Hence he does not grieve, is not depressed, does not lament, beating his breast, or weep and fall into bewilderment. Thus, monk, is there lack of anxiety about external things that do not exist."

"Lord, can there be anxiety about inner things that do not exist?"

"There can be, monk," said the Blessed One. "In such cases, monk, someone has this [Upaniṣadic] view: 'All this is the Self. That I shall be after death; permanent, stable, eternal, immutable; eternally the same, I shall abide in that very condition.'[1] He then hears a Tathāgata expounding the teaching for the removal of all grounds for views, of all prejudices, obsessions, dogmas, and biases; for the stilling of all (karmic) processes, for the relinquishment of all substrata (of existence), for the extirpation of craving, for dispassion, cessation, nirvāna. He then thinks: 'I shall be annihilated, I shall be destroyed! No longer shall I exist!' Hence he grieves, is depressed and laments; beating his breast, he weeps, and falls into bewilderment. Thus, monk, is there anxiety about inner things that do not exist."

"But, Lord, can there be absence of anxiety about inner things that do not exist?"

"There can be, monk," said the Blessed One. "In that case, monk, someone does not have this [Upaniṣadic] view 'All this is the Self. That I shall be after death; permanent, stable, eternal, immutable; eternally the same, I shall abide in that very condition.' He then hears a Tathāgata expounding the teaching for the removal of all grounds for views, of all prejudices, obsessions, dogmas, and biases; for the stilling of all (karmic) processes, for the relinquishment of all substrata (of existence), for the extirpation of craving, for dispassion, cessation, nirvāna. He does not then think: 'I shall be annihilated, I shall be destroyed! No longer shall I exist!' Hence he does not grieve, is not depressed, and does not lament, beating his breast, or weeps, and

---

1. This is a view of the nature of the self that is found in some of the Upaniṣads, which are the final portion of the Vedas (the sacred texts of the orthodox Brahmanical schools). As interpreted by the later Advaita Vedānta school, it claims that the true self of the individual is not distinct from the pure Being ("all this") that underlies all apparent diversity in the world. It is but one of many different views about the self and its nature that the Buddha rejects. It is possible that the Buddha singles out this particular view here because it was held by one of the interlocutors in the discussion.

fall into bewilderment. Thus, monk, is there absence of anxiety about internal things that do not exist." . . .

"What do you think, monks: Is *rūpa* permanent or impermanent?"[2]—"Impermanent, Lord."—"And what is impermanent, is it painful or pleasant?"—"Painful, Lord."—"What is impermanent, painful, subject to change, is it fit to be considered mine, me, my self?"—"Certainly not, Lord."—"What do you think, monks: Is feeling . . . is perception . . . are dispositions . . . is consciousness . . . permanent or impermanent?"—"Impermanent, Lord."—"And what is impermanent, is it painful or pleasant?"—"Painful, Lord."—"And what is impermanent, painful, subject to change, is it fit to be considered mine, me, my self?"—"Certainly not, Lord." . . .

"Therefore, monks, give up whatever is not yours. Your giving it up will bring you welfare and happiness for a long time. What is it that is not yours? *Rūpa* is not yours. Give it up! Your giving it up will for a long time bring you welfare and happiness. Feeling is not yours. Give it up! Your giving it up will bring you welfare and happiness for a long time. Perception is not yours. Give it up! Your giving it up will bring you welfare and happiness for a long time. Dispositions are not yours. Give them up! Your giving them up will bring you welfare and happiness for a long time. Consciousness is not yours. Give it up! Your giving it up will bring you welfare and happiness for a long time.

"What do you think, monks: If people were to carry off the grass, sticks, branches, and leaves in this Jeta Grove,[3] or burnt them or did with them whatever they pleased, would you think: These people carry us off, or burn us, or do with us as they please?"—"No, Lord."—"Why

---

2. *Rūpa* is the first of the five *skandha*s or groups of psychophysical elements, the parts out of which persons are composed. It represents the physical side of our existence, the parts of our bodies. The other four are feeling, perception, dispositions, and consciousness. This paragraph contains condensed versions of two arguments for the non-existence of the self, arguments that are discussed in detail in Chapter 2.

3. The setting of this and many other discourses.

not?" Because, Lord, those things are neither our self nor what belongs to our self."—"So, too, monks, give up what is not yours! Your giving it up will bring you welfare and happiness for a long time. What is it that is not yours? *Rūpa* . . . feeling . . . perception . . . dispositions . . . consciousness are not yours. Give them up! Your giving them up will bring you welfare and happiness for a long time."

Supplementary Reading for Chapter 2

Translated from Buddhaghosa's *Visuddhimagga* XVII.162–72

The author of this passage, Buddhaghosa, is one of the most important philosophers of the Theravāda school of Abhidharma. While it was written many centuries after the death of the Buddha, the passage represents the consensus view of how rebirth may be possible without a transmigrating self. Buddhaghosa uses the common seed-fruit metaphor for the karmic process: a seed is produced by the performance of an intentional action, and its fruit is the pleasant or painful experience that is eventually produced as a result. The passage addresses the same question that Nāgasena discussed in the excerpt from Milindapañha presented in Chapter 2, §8, but it uses different examples to illustrate the process. Also new here is the claim that the person in the new life and the person in the prior life are "neither the same nor different." In examining this passage, it may be useful to consider how the distinction between conventional truth and ultimate truth bears on its interpretation.

It is only elements of being possessing a dependence that arrive at a new existence: none transmigrated from the last existence, nor are they in the new existence without causes contained in the old. By this is said that it is only elements of being, with *rūpa* or without, but possessing a dependence, that arrive at a new existence. There is no entity, no living principle; no elements of being transmigrated from the last existence into the present one; nor, on the other hand, do they appear in the present existence without causes in that one. This we will now make plain by considering birth and death as they occur every day among people.

For when, in any existence, one arrives at the gate of death, either in the natural course of things or through violence; and when, by a concourse of intolerable, death-dealing pains, all the members, both great and small, are loosened and wrenched apart in every joint and ligament; and the body, like a green palm-leaf exposed to the sun, dries up by degrees; and the eyesight and the other senses fail; and the power of feeling, and the power of thinking, and vitality are making the last stand in the heart—then consciousness residing in that last refuge, the heart, continues to exist by virtue of karma, otherwise called the dispositions. This karma, however, still retains something of what it depends on, and consists of such former deeds as were weighty, much practiced, and are now close at hand; or else this karma creates a reflex of itself or of the new mode of life now being entered upon, and it is with this as its object that consciousness continues to exist.

Now while the consciousness still subsists, inasmuch as desire and ignorance have not been abandoned and the evil of the object is hidden by that ignorance, desire inclines the consciousness to the object; and the karma that sprang up along with the consciousness impels it toward the object. This consciousness being in its series thus inclined toward the object by desire, and impelled toward it by karma, like someone who swings themselves over a ditch by means of a rope hanging from a tree on the hither bank, quits its first resting place and continues to subsist in dependence on objects of sense and other things, and either does or does not light on another resting place created by karma. Here the former consciousness, from its passing out of existence, is called passing away, and the latter, from its being reborn into a new existence, is called rebirth. But it is to be understood that this latter consciousness did not come to the present existence from the previous one, and also that it is only to causes contained in the old existence—namely, to karma called the dispositions, to inclination, an object, etc.—that its present appearance is due.

> As illustrations here may serve
>
> Echoes and other similes.
>
> Neither sameness nor diversity,
>
> Can from that series take their rise.

As illustrations of how consciousness does not come over from the last existence into the present, and how it springs up by means of causes belonging to the former existence, here may serve echoes, light, the impressions of a seal, and reflections in a mirror. For as echoes, light, the impressions of a seal, and shadows have sound, etc., for their causes, and exist without having come from elsewhere, just so is it with this mind.

Moreover

> Neither sameness, nor diversity,
>
> Can from that series take their rise.

For if, in a continuous series, an absolute sameness obtained, then could sour cream not arise from milk; while, on the other hand, if there were an absolute diversity, then could not a milk-owner obtain sour cream. The same argument holds good in regard to all causes and effects. This being so, it would be more correct not to use the popular mode of stating the case, but that would not be desirable. Therefore, we must merely guard ourselves from supposing that there is here either an absolute sameness or an absolute diversity. Here someone will object,

"This explanation is not a good one. For is it not true that if there be no transmigration, and both the *skandha*s and the fruitful karma which belong to this existence in the world of men cease, nor arrive in the new existence, the fruit of this karma would then be borne by a different thing from that which produced the karma itself? And if there is no reaper, who is it that experiences the fruit? Therefore this position is not good."

The following quotation will answer this:

> "The series which bears fruit,
>
> Is not the same nor something else.
>
> The fabricating power in seeds
>
> Will show the meaning of this word."

For when the fruit arises in a series, as identity and distinctness [of person] are both excluded, it cannot be said that the fruit is borne by the same thing nor yet by something else.

The fabricating power in seeds will show this. For when the fabricating power in the seed of mangoes and other plants operate, inasmuch as any particular kind of fruit is dependent on the previous part of its series, it cannot come from other seeds, nor in dependence on other fabricating powers; nor yet is it those other seeds, or those other fabricating powers, which arrive at fruition. Such is to be understood to be the nature of the present case. Also when education, training, and medicaments have been applied to the body of a young person, the fruit will appear after time in the mature body, etc. Thus is the sense to be understood.

Now as to what was said, "If there is no reaper, who is it that experiences the fruit?" consider the following:

> "As when it is said, 'The tree bears fruit,'
>
> As soon as fruit appears on it;
>
> Just so the *skandha*s are called reapers,
>
> As soon as karma's fruit arises."

Just as in the case of those elements of being which go under the name of tree, as soon as at any point the fruit springs up, it is then said, "The tree bears fruit," or, "The tree has fructified"—so also in the case of those *skandha*s which go under the name of "god" or "man," when a fruition of happiness or misery springs up at any point, then it is said, "That god or man is happy or miserable." Therefore is it that we have here no need of any superfluous reaper.

Supplementary Reading for Chapter 3

Translated from Prajñākaramati's commentary *Pañjikā* on Śāntideva's *Bodhicaryāvatāra* 6.22–39

This passage is from a later Mahāyāna text that describes various practices designed to help one develop the virtues of a bodhisattva (someone destined to become a buddha). The chapter from which this is excerpted, Chapter 6, is devoted to the development of patience toward those who have inflicted harm on us; it is concerned, in other words, with learning how to keep from getting angry. We ordinarily think anger at someone is justified when the harm they have inflicted is intentional; in such cases, we think the person is blameworthy. Given that blame and praise are connected to the idea of moral responsibility, this means that the discussion may have some bearing on the question of determinism and moral responsibility that was discussed in Chapter 3, §5. Remember that the resolution of the Buddhist "free will" problem presented in Chapter 3 was said to be one of several possible approaches a Buddhist non-self theorist could take. Does this passage support the approach of that resolution or does it conflict with it?

> 6.22. I feel no anger towards bile and the like, even though they cause intense suffering. Why am I angry with sentient beings? They too have causes for their anger.

The body is subject to defects in the three humors of bile, etc. When there are difficulties in supplying or removing the humors, they can bring about a troubled condition of piercing pain. Yet, I am not angry at them, for this is not intentional. They did not bring about suffering upon reflection. Why is this? They became irritated through an aggregate of intrinsic causal factors. This being so, then why should there be anger at what does have intentions [i.e., persons who act on their desires]? Why shouldn't there be? Because they likewise bring about suffering having been irritated by an aggregate of intrinsic causal factors due to prior bad actions. So they are no more deserving of my anger than bile and the like. In both cases, there is the same property of being subject to causation.

> 23. Just as that stomach pain arises unwished for,
>
> So anger arises unwished for from power.

Just as it is due to the capacities arisen from their own conditions that bile, etc., though devoid of intention, necessarily bring about stomach pain, so likewise, anger arises through the ill-minded power obtained through transformation of its own cause. The two cases are alike in both being subject to cause and conditions.

Here it might be objected that since intentional beings are capable of reflection, they are the agents of wished-for effects. But this is also not so, as he says:

> 24. Someone does not get angry voluntarily out of their own desire, thinking "I will be angry."
>
> And anger does not arise upon the intention "Let it arise."

A person does not become angry willfully, having the prior thought, "I am angry," without the aggregate of conditions. And anger does not arise autonomously with the aim of bringing itself forth. Thus the following is established as proven:

> 25. Whatever actions there are, be they offenses, evil deeds, or otherwise, they all occur through the power of their conditions and not autonomously.

Everything has the intrinsic nature of having occurred solely due to the conditions for its arising. Neither is there found anything that is commenced autonomously.

26. Nor does the aggregate of conditions think, "I will produce."

Neither does what is produced think, "I have been produced."

Although the aggregate of conditions is sufficient for the production of its effect, it is not the case that it produces intentionally. For it produces an effect of such a nature by virtue of what is deposited through the transformation of itself as cause, but not intentionally. Neither does the produced effect attend to the thought, "I have been produced by that aggregate." Thus all *dharma*s are devoid of [conscious] operation.[4] In which case, here is how things are: due to the origination of x, y comes to be. This world is nothing but the conditionality of something on something else. No autonomy is possible, due to the dependence of all *dharma*s on causes and conditions.

Perhaps it will be said that autonomy is to be found in the primary cause of the Sāṃkhya school, or the self or space and the like as posited by the Nyāya school.[5] Doubting this, he replies that no autonomy whatsoever is found there:

27. This primary cause that is posited, this self that is imagined,

Certainly these do not arise thinking "I will exist."

---

4. A *dharma* is an ultimately real entity. More has been said about *dharma*s in Chapter 4.

5. If, as has been argued so far, the effect of a prior cause cannot be autonomous and so an appropriate target of anger, perhaps something not subject to causation, something eternal, might be. Sāṃkhya and Vaiśeṣika, two orthodox Brahmanical schools, both claim that there are eternally existing things. One such thing for Sāṃkhya is the "primary cause" (*prakṛti*), a neutral stuff out of which the world evolved. For Vaiśeṣika (and its sister school Nyāya), selves and space are examples of eternal substances.

The primary cause is thought to be *prakṛti*, the three elementary properties of *sattva*, *rajas*, and *tamas* in the state of equilibrium. In saying
"certainly," he reveals the unwanted consequence that this is without
proof. And anything whatsoever that is imagined or judged to be the
self is also without proof. For it is just itself since it is devoid of causing
anything else, it does not come into existence thinking, "Originating,
I shall exist." As for why,

> 28ab. For what is unarisen there is no [originating], what
> wish to come to be could there be?

For this primary cause and the like, there is only prior non-existence,
as with the child of a barren woman, how could there be a wish to exist
and arise? Nothing non-existent arises. Origination is always just the
transformation from the unmanifest to the manifest state. Or, if such
transformation is also non-existent, how does it originate the manifest
state? And there is also the absurd consequence that its arising is from
the manifest state of transformation, that being its intrinsic nature.
Without it, there is lack of connection. If a connection is posited, there
is infinite regress. The primary cause has been extensively refuted.

But perhaps these faults do not affect the self. "We do not posit
its arising. It is eternal, being by nature permanent, it is unarisen."
Of course, this is what you (Naiyāyikas) will say. And accordingly,
because it does not arise, it is in all respects just like the horns of a
donkey. Consequently it is not dealt with here.

That which is unoriginated does not exist; how can there then
be the wish to arise? Even if it exists, it still lacks the capacity in itself.
For it [the self as subject of the desire for the object] is fundamentally
inclined toward the object. And so, prior to attainment of the object,
it will lack the nature of agent of enjoyment. And after origination,
just that [being the subject of enjoyment] is its nature, for otherwise it
would be unsuited for the role of enjoyer. And if there is its arising, why
is this "the arising of it" not to be considered the arising of the self?
This is why it was said,

> For what is unarisen there is no [originating], what wish to come to be could there be?

And there are yet other defects:

> 28cd. And since it is engrossed in its object, it is not able to cease.

Suppose what you hold is that it functions for the enjoyment of objects occurring in the primary cause. Then it cannot be the case that there is the subsequent functioning of what previously did not function. And then how can consciousness function? Consequently, there would be no stopping of its being engrossed in the object. Just as he says, it is not able to cease. It is not capable of stopping its enjoying of the object, for that is then its intrinsic nature, that being ceaseless due to its permanence. Were it to stop, it would absurdly follow that it was impermanent. And the doctrine of the self of the Naiyāyikas has it that it is permanent.

There is also its characteristic mark:

> 29ab. Something that is by nature permanent and insentient is clearly devoid of activity, like space.

The characteristic mark of Sāṃkhya's primary cause is its being unconscious; elsewhere, the mark is said to be homogeneity. To be permanent is to have the same intrinsic nature both earlier and later. And to be insentient is to be intrinsically unconscious, meaning inert. It is due to connection with a distinct consciousness that it is perceived, like the all-pervading sky. So it is clearly evident that it is inactive. So it is said,

> Others posit a self that is the substrate of desire, etc., that is not itself conscious, and is permanent and all-pervasive,
>
> The agents of good and bad deeds and the reaper of their fruit, distinct from consciousness and not intrinsically conscious.[6]

---

6. In order to account for the occurrence of dreamless sleep, Nyāya claims that the self is not always conscious. Like a glass ball that may be either colored or colorless depending on conditions, the self is sometimes modified by desire, or by activity, or by awareness, etc., but in itself, it is none of those modes.

Consequently, due to lack of contact, there being no deed and nowhere an effect, it is not an agent. It is only due to contact with concomitant conditions that action is metaphorically attributed to what is devoid of action. As is said elsewhere, its being called an agent is due to its connection with cognition, effort, and the like.

> 29cd. Even in conjunction with distinct conditions, how can something that effects no change be active?

Even when there is concomitance with cognition, effort, and other distinct conditions, what action can there be for a self that has not lost its original intrinsic nature of being devoid of activity due to its permanence? Not at all is it right to say there is activity.

> 30. What part of an action is done by something that remains the same as before?
>
> There being a connection expressed as "its action," which of the two (the self or the conditions) is the cause of that act?

Something that is just the same at the time of the action as it was earlier, what part of an action is done by that when it is deprived of the intrinsic nature of a doer? And because of the absence of connection between the two, where it is said that this is the action of the self, which is it, the self or something else, that is the efficient cause?

It is widely held that no autonomy whatsoever is possible with respect to the self, Īśvara, and other things characterized by the lack of intending to bring something about.[7] Accordingly, to show the universal absence of real autonomy, he says,

> 31. Thus everything is through the power of something else, which is in turn not self-caused.
>
> The behavior of beings is like a magic show; what is one angry at?

---

7. According to some orthodox schools, this world was created by an eternal omniscient being, Īśvara.

Accordingly, all originated things, whether external or internal to the person, are brought about by the power of something else, subject to another. Suppose it is objected that there surely must be something whose power does not derive from something else. We reply that there is not. The power of that which determines something else is in turn dependent on its own cause. And so, even for the cause of its cause, in the beginningless wheel of saṃsāra nothing self-caused is possible. And so, all *dharma*s are devoid of activity. Who is it ultimately who inflicts harm by means of what? Hatred is appropriate with respect to that for which there is some wrongdoer who committed some wrong. So just as with a magic show, all thoughts of activity are dissipated. All *dharma*s being without desire or intent, at what should one get angry? It is never justified for the wise, no matter what the hurt.

Here someone else, reflecting on this, raises an objection:

> 32ab. Resisting anger is equally inappropriate, for who resists what?

By the same reasoning, resisting and refraining [from anger, hatred, desire, etc.] are not appropriate with respect to animate beings, just like nirvāna, since there is no autonomy to be found. Everything arises dependent on an aggregate of conditions. So resisting anger is likewise inappropriate. Why is this? What autonomous agent resists what autonomously commenced state that is to be rejected? Here is what we mean. Doesn't the same reasoning apply to refraining as to commencing? So by the same reasoning, resisting is never right.

If this is what you think, here is his reply:

> 32cd. It is appropriate, for the stopping of suffering is thought to be dependent on conditions.

Resisting is appropriate. Why? Because of conditionality. This arises in dependence on that: since there is also dependent origination in the case of animate beings, resisting is appropriate. Hence there is no inconsistency. If it is the case that all *dharma*s are without [conscious] operation, it is nonetheless also true that because of dependent origination, they are said to be heteronomous. For it is said that all are so by the power of another. Thus due to the power of conditions consisting of ignorance, etc. [in the twelve-linked chain of dependent origination], there proceeds, one after another, a stream of effects in the form of dispositions. There is the stopping of one by the stopping of its predecessor. This has all been explained extensively elsewhere. This is how the cessation, the stopping of the suffering of saṃsāra, is understood. Hence one engages in resistance to engaging in the vices of hatred, etc. In dependence on that, there arises the appropriate result whose nature is to be the greatest possible happiness.

He now applies this to the case at hand.

> 33. Consequently, when someone is seen doing something wrong, whether it is a friend or a foe,
>
> Reflecting that this has its own particular causes, be content.

Since everything arises in dependence, the stance that should be taken toward the wrongdoer, whether foe or otherwise, is just contentment. Why? The causes of the wrongdoing are meritorious regardless of whether it was done by friend or otherwise. So, of course, one should be content. There is no doing out of evil intent. Even where there is a mental disturbance caused by some sort of sudden, painful attack, this is not the stopping of suffering, as he explains:

> 34. If all living beings attained their wishes,
>
> No one would suffer; no one wishes for suffering.

Not by means of just one's own desire does one prevent what is unwished for or bring about what is wished for, but rather by means of a distinct cause. Accordingly, what is wished for is that there be no suffering of anyone. How is this? No one wishes for their own suffering. All beings are desirous of their own happiness.

Having explained impatience at being infused with pain, he now proceeds to explain patience as forbearance in the face of the wrongs of another.

> 35. Due to their own delusion, they harm themselves with thorns and the like,
>
> Because of their gluttony, anger, lust for unattainable partners, etc.

> 36. Some kill themselves by hanging, throwing themselves off a cliff, ingesting poison or other harmful things, and by doing bad deeds.

> 37. When due to the power of the defilements (desire, hatred, and delusion) they can destroy even their own dear selves,
>
> How can they avoid doing so to the bodies of others?

Delusion is the result of not investigating thoroughly. . . . When these beings hurt and harm even their own dear and beloved self in such ways because of the power of the defilements, due to the heteronomy of the defilements, why would there be the cessation of harming others' bodies?

Such beings are deserving of pity, not hatred.

> 38. Why is it that not only is there no pity toward those who, made mad by the defilements, kill themselves, but even anger arises?

These offenders are like those possessed by demons. Whether it is by harming themselves or by harming others, in neither case is there pity. But here, the indifference of sages is not right. Why does hatred arise? The state of pity is the great antidote. And so accordingly let anger be kept from one's mind:

39. If it is the nature of the ignorant to act violently toward others,

Then it is not appropriate for me to be angry at them, any more than it would make sense to feel anger at fire for burning oneself.

Supplementary Reading for Chapter 4, §2

Translated from Vasubandhu's *Abhidharmkakośabhāṣya* on *Abhidharma-kośa* IV.2c–3b

In this passage, the philosopher Vasubandhu presents the main argument that Vaibhāṣika used to support the doctrine of momentariness, the view that entities cease existing immediately after they arise. The passage starts and ends with the claim that strictly speaking, nothing ever moves, which is a consequence of the doctrine of momentariness. (In the time between an entity's being at A and an entity's being at B, the entity that was at A will have gone out of existence.) But the focus of the passage is the argument for momentariness. Since this is the argument that was discussed in Chapter 4, §2, reading this passage will give you an opportunity to compare the original and the modern interpretation.

2c. There is no going, since the conditioned is momentary,

What is this "moment?" Immediate cessation upon having obtained existence. What exists in this fashion is momentary. Indeed nothing conditioned exists later than its acquisition of existence. It perishes just where it was born. Its movement to another place would be impossible. Thus there is no bodily action of going.

[Objection:] This would be so if universal momentariness were proven.

[Reply:] It is proven that conditioned things are momentary. How? With respect to the conditioned, necessarily,

2d. Because it perishes.

For the cessation of conditioned things is spontaneous. Why is this? A cause is of an effect. And cessation is an absence. What is there to be done with respect to an absence? Therefore destruction does not depend on a cause. If it were not so with respect to what has just arisen, there would likewise be no destruction later, for it would still be the same.

[Objection:] But an existing thing changes [so it can go out of existence later, in dependence on its changed state].

[Reply:] It is wrong to say of something that that very thing can be otherwise. For how is it possible that it itself is different from that?

[Objection:] But surely it is seen that there is destruction of wood and the like due to contact with fire, etc. And there is no means of knowledge more important than perception. Not all cessation is spontaneous—how can you think, "I see the cessation of wood and the like due to contact with fire and the like?"

[Reply:] Because one doesn't see them [being destroyed by contact with fire and the like]. This is to be reflected upon: Is it that wood, etc., are not seen because they were destroyed due to contact with fire etc., or that they are not seen because, they having themselves ceased, others have not arisen in their place? As with a lamp [that has been blown out] through contact with the wind or the sound of a bell [that has stopped] through contact with the hand. Therefore this matter is to be decided through inference.

[Objection:] But what is the inference here?

[Reply:] As was already said, because an absence is not an effect. Moreover,

3a. Not without a cause would anything [cease]

If cessation were universally due to a cause, then nothing whatsoever would stop without a cause, such as origination. The cessation of momentary things such as thoughts, sounds, and flames is seen to be spontaneous; it does not depend on a cause. As for the notion that the cessation of a thought is due to another thought, that of a sound is due to another sound, that is wrong. For the two thoughts do not occur together. For there is no mutual contact of the states of doubt and certainty, of pleasure and pain, of desire and hate. And when a strong thought or sound is followed by a weak thought or sound, why would the weak *dharma* destroy a stronger one of the same kind? If it is thought with respect to the last two cases that cessation is due to the absence of a cause of persistence of flames or due to virtue and vice, that is incorrect. For absence is not capable of being a cause. And the prevention of occurrence or obtaining from moment to moment of the arising and cessation of virtue and vice is not possible. It is possible to apply this reasoning to all constructed things, so enough of this discussion.

If, moreover, the cessation of wood and the like were because of contact with fire and the like, then in the arising of qualities produced by heating in what is more and more heated,

3b. The cause would also be the destroyer.

Why is that? Either those heat-produced qualities that are arisen in grass and the like through relation to fire are just due to what is thus, or else their destruction is in the arising of the more and more heated, precisely the cause would be their destroyer, there would be no difference in causes. And it is not right that what their existence is from should also be just what their non-existence is from. That would be to imagine that within flames, there are distinct causes.

[Objection:] What is it that is thus constructed in the case of the arising of heat-produced differences through connection of lye, snow, acid, sun, and the watery? In the case of boiling water that grows less, what is it that contact with heat does there?

[Reply:] By virtue of its contact with fire, through the force of the fire, the heat element—which is present in water—increases; and increasing, causes the mass of water to be reborn in quantities more and more reduced, until being totally reduced, the series does not renew itself. This is what contact with fire does to water. Therefore, there is no cause for the destruction of things; it is just intrinsic. Ceasing because of their transitoriness, being just arisen they go out of existence. Destruction in an instant is thus proven, and from destruction in a moment, the absence of motion is proven. There is the conception of movement, however, when there is an uninterrupted arising in different locations, as with a grass fire.

Supplementary Reading for Chapter 4, §5

Translated from *Vijñaptimātratāsiddhi* (*Viṃśatikā*) of Vasubandhu, verses 11–14

The author of the text from which this passage is excerpted is the same Vasubandhu who wrote the preceding supplementary reading on momentariness. But whereas that text was written from the standpoint of the Vaibhāṣika school, this text is written in support of Yogācāra idealism. Its title, Vijñaptimātratāsiddhi, *means "The proof that there are only impressions (or mental states)." In this excerpt Vasubandhu presents one important argument for idealism, the argument from the infinite divisibility of material things. It starts by asking what exactly it is that we are aware of when we see a patch of color, feel an occurrence of hardness or smoothness, and so on, if, as the realist assumes, those experiences are caused by physical objects such as pots. If a pot is really just many atoms arranged in a certain way, then it can't be the pot that is what we see (since wholes are not ultimately real), nor is it the individual atoms (which are too small to see). The remaining option that the many atoms work together as an aggregate to cause the sensations, is the chief target of Vasubandhu's argument. It may be worth considering whether his argument creates genuine difficulties for those who believe there really is an external world.*

> 11. That is not one, nor is the object a plurality made up of atoms,
>
> Neither do they aggregate, since the atom is unproven.

What is mean by this? If the *āyatanas*[8] of color-and-shape, etc., were respectively the objects of impressions of color-and-shape, etc., then they would be individuals, like the "whole" posited by the Vaiśeṣikas,[9] or they would be pluralities made up of atoms, or they would themselves be the aggregates of atoms. But the object is not an individual since one never apprehends a whole that is distinct from its parts. Neither is it a plurality, since one does not apprehend atoms individually. Nor, finally, do the aggregates [of atoms] become the object of perception since there is no proof that the atom is an individual substance.

Why is it not proven? Because,

> 12ab. The atom must have six parts, for it joins simultaneously with six others.

The atom will have six parts if it joins simultaneously with six atoms from six sides since it is impossible that where one is another should be.

---

8. The *āyatana* classification is an alternative to the *skandhas* classification. The twelve *āyatanas* are vision and visible things (color-and-shape), hearing and sounds, etc. The opponent has just claimed that since the Buddha taught that there are twelve *āyatanas*, his authority must stand behind the belief in physical objects. He would not have taught that such things as colored patches exist if he did not hold that there is an external world containing things with colors and shapes.

9. Vaiśeṣika is an orthodox school. It claims that a whole such as a chariot is something that exists over and above its parts.

12cd. [Otherwise] it would be a mass having the size of one atom, because all six would be in the same place.

Or else the space [occupied by] one atom is that of all six. Then because all are in the same place, they would all together be a mass the size of one atom; then because of lack of mutual separation, no mass whatever would be visible.

[The opponent:] The atoms do not at all unite since they are partless. Hence the fault does not arise as a consequence [of our position]. Aggregates, however, do join. So say the Vaibhāṣikas of Kashmir.

They should be replied to as follows: the aggregate of atoms is not an object distinct from those [atoms].

13. If the atoms do not join, then with respect to their aggregates, of what is there this [joining]?

It cannot be shown that their joining does not take place because of their partlessness.

Suppose that the aggregated things do not join with one another. Then it should be pointed out that it is not right to deny joining on the grounds of the partlessness of the atoms since one could not then acknowledge the joining of the aggregate, even though it has parts. Thus it does not follow that the atom is a distinct substance. Moreover, regardless of whether one allows that atoms join or not,

14. There is no individuality of that which can be divided into distinct spatial parts.

On the opposite assumption, why is there shade and obstruction? If the mass is not distinct, these two do not characterize it.

In other words, if there are distinct spatial parts of the atom, such as the east part, the upper part, etc., then how should there be any individuality of an atom with such a nature?

If each atom has no distinct spatial parts, then how is it that upon the appearance of the sun, in one place there is shade, in another there is sunlight? There would be no place at which it is different from where the sunlight is. And how can there be obstructing of one atom by another if distinct spatial parts are not posited? The atom has no other parts whatever where, by having come there, it could be resisted by another. Then as has been said [above], in the absence of resistance, the entire aggregate would be the size of an atom since all would occupy the same place.

[Objection:] Why not say this, that shade and obstruction pertain to the mass, not to the atom?

[Reply:] What mass could possibly be posited as distinct from the atoms yet characterized by these two [shade and obstruction]? None, and thus it is said, "If the mass is not something distinct, these two do not characterize it." That is, if the mass is not posited as something distinct from the atoms, then these two will not characterize it.

[Objection:] The atom, the aggregate, and the like, are fabricated constructions, what is the point of considering them when the characteristics of color-and-shape cannot be denied?

[Reply:] What, then, are their characteristics?

[The opponent:] The property of being the object of vision, etc., and blueness, etc.

[Reply:] That is precisely what is being deliberated upon, whether what is taken to be the object of vision, etc., is a single substance or a plurality.

Index